DATE DUE

Also by James Carville

All's Fair
(with Mary Matalin)

We're Right, They're Wrong

...And the Horse He Rode In On

He Rode In On

The People v. Kenneth Starr

James Carville

Simon & Schuster

To R. Todd De Lorenzo, who means so much to me
and my family, and
to Mark Weiner, whom I've slept with many a night
(don't subpoena me, Ken—they were airplane
flights to Latin America!)

 SIMON & SCHUSTER
Rockefeller Center
1230 Avenue of the Americas
New York, NY 10020

Copyright © 1998 by James Carville

Designed by Sam Potts

Manufactured in the United States of America

1 3 5 7 9 10 8 6 4 2

Library of Congress
Cataloging-in-Publication Data is available.

ISBN 0-684-85734-0

Acknowledgments

In *All's Fair*, I didn't want to have any acknowledgments because I would invariably leave someone out and end up making a friend angry. In *We're Right, They're Wrong*, I forgot my own advice and acknowledged people, and yes, we left out some folks who got mad.

So I will acknowledge the magnificent work of Kevin Murphy, a great guy and a great collaborator; Geoffrey Kloske and his colleagues at Simon & Schuster; and all the people who have fought so hard and so passionately for the ideas and ideals that we share.

In closing, I also must mention David Rosenthal, who pays me; Bob Barnett, who represents me; and Alice Mayhew, who inspires me.

"The President's attackers are a motley band, consisting primarily of perjuring partisan politicians, strumpets, hags, bitter old segregationists, hired guns for cigarette companies, felons, judges who trade favors for jobs, bitter, defeated, pathetic former political rivals, Hillary-hating misogynists, wacko billionaires, gay-bashers, hate radio hucksters, mother-subpoenaing prosecutors, and mother-suing nutcases, all feeding an endless line of lies and half-truths to jealous journalists, envious editorialists, curmudgeonly columnists, and cranky commentators more concerned with their own self-importance and trashing the good name of a great President than the truth."

—*James Carville*

Contents

"Just the facts, ma'am, just the facts."

—Jack Webb, from *Dragnet*,
as quoted by Kenneth Starr
on 4/2/98

Introduction:

I Meet the Independent Counsel

You know something? I don't like Ken Starr.

I don't like one damn thing about him. I don't like his politics. I don't like his sanctimony. I don't like his self-piety. I don't like the people he runs with. I don't like his suck-up, spit-down view of the world, how he kisses up to the powerful and abuses the life out of regular people. I don't like his private legal clients. I don't like the folks who work for him—or the people who apologize for him, either. I don't like the way he always smiles at the wrong time. (I never trust a person a smile doesn't come naturally to.) I don't like the way he always compares himself—favorably, of course—to cherished American icons. And I absolutely won't stand for the way he has single-handedly demeaned the Constitution of our great nation. No American should.

Now, don't get me wrong, I don't *hate* the guy. I don't wish him personal ill. I just flat out do not like him. I think he's an abusive, privacy-invading, sex-obsessed, right-wing, constitutionally insensitive, boring, obsequious, and miserable little man who has risen further in this life by his willingness to suck up to power than his meager talents and pitiful judgment ever would have gotten him. I wouldn't want to have a beer with him—if I did, he'd probably subpoena the waitress. If I were forced to, I'd be cool and civil to him, like you might act toward a crazy brother-in-law at a family picnic. But you'll still never catch me shaking hands with him and saying, "Aw, shucks, it's all just business, Ken."

That's only an indication of my intense distaste—not hatred—of the man.

Let me say this—there are a lot of Republicans I do like (heck, I'm married to one). I remain on friendly terms with any number of GOP lawmakers, right-wing journalists, and conservative political operatives. Indubitably, I can disagree with someone politically without being disagreeable to them personally, and even admire them as friends and human beings. But for more reasons than a good bookkeeper could ever tote up, Ken Starr rubs me the wrong way.

Now, you might think my dislike of the independent counsel has something to do with this whole Monica Lewinsky imbroglio—and you'd be right about that. You might also surmise that I can't stand Ken Starr because of his four-year, $40 million joke of a Whitewater investigation. Well, that's true too. But in fact most of my contempt for Inspector Starr predates all of his current silly, worthless, and ridiculously expensive hatchet jobs.

That independent counsel of ours has stuck in my craw for some time now.

I'm concerned that if we somehow let this man continue his jihad against the President, my worst sweat-sheet nightmare will actually come true: Ken Starr will never go away. The mean and menacing essence of him will remain with us forever like Strom Thurmond or a cheap tattoo. And whenever the right wing doesn't like a popularly elected official such as President Clinton, they'll throw plenty of lies and money around just to get their way.

Many of you know that I've been calling foul for a long time when it comes to Mr. Starr. From the moment he slid into place four long years ago (can you believe this joker has been around longer than George Bush?), this independent counsel has smelled funky. From the start of this whole mess, I've been working to get the facts about Ken Starr out. And now that Mr. Starr has the whole country's attention with his bag of dirty tricks, I feel an even more pressing obligation to make a clear case explaining why the independent counsel's investigation is nothing more than a partisan, fanatical plan to bring down the democratically elected President of the United States.

That's just plain wrong, and that's why I had to write this book. I wanted to put all the nasty facts about Mr. Starr in one place where everyone can finally see what a travesty of justice, and mammoth waste of taxpayer—your—money, his investigation is.

* * *

You know, for a guy who talks all the time, I seem to be misunderstood by an awful lot of people. Ever since I started telling the

American public about the partisan abuses of Kenneth Starr, when I created the Education and Information Project (EIP) back in 1996, many people in the media and on the political right have maligned my motives regarding the independent counsel. Since I first voiced my disapproving opinion of Mr. Starr, members of the press have had a field day calling me names, including "rabid dog," "court jester," "clown," and, one of my personal favorites, "Aging Enfant Terrible in Midlife Crisis."[1] Even my sweet wife, Mary, calls me a serpenthead.

Some folks have even tried to silence me with threats of hearings and investigations. Representative Bob Barr, the Georgia Republican and the House of Representatives' resident impeachment fanatic,* called for public hearings on me because I was trying "to influence ongoing judicial proceedings by impugning the integrity of the chief prosecutor."[2] Mark Levin of the Landmark Legal Foundation, one of the many right-wing groups subsidized by anti-Clinton billionaire Richard Mellon Scaife, asked Attorney General Janet Reno to bring me up on obstruction of justice charges. And Larry Klayman of Judicial Watch (you guessed it, another right-wing Scaife-funded outfit) has subpoenaed every single piece of paper in my office, including such incriminating documents as my back copies of *Time* and *Newsweek* magazines, all in the hopes of shutting me up.

And, right after the national media became obsessed with

---

* Yes, this is the same Bob Barr who authored the Defense of Marriage Act and who has been married three times.

...And the Horse He Rode In On

Monica Lewinsky this past January, it became fashionable once again among Washington journalists to accuse me of being a "junkyard dog" for the White House, vilifying the motives of the honorable Judge Starr merely to obstruct his so-called "impartial" investigation.

Well, those schoolyard tactics won't slow me down one bit. My contempt for this particular independent counsel started long before most of the world had ever heard of Monica Lewinsky or Linda Tripp, or even of Inspector Starr. In fact, my problems with this man began almost five years ago, in October of 1993, when Ken Starr was just a poisonous gleam in Jesse Helms's eye.

That was just before my wedding to Ms. Mary Matalin. I was waiting for the love of my life at Washington National Airport. Mary was returning from making a speech in Hartford, Connecticut, and (as I found out later would be business as usual) she was running late.

So there I was at the USAir Club, sipping on a cup of coffee, thumbing through the sports pages, checking to see how the LSU Tigers were doing, when I noticed an intense, bespectacled man sidling up to me. I didn't recognize the guy, but I figured I might have met him somewhere along the 1992 campaign trail, so I gave him a nod and flashed him a big, friendly Serpenthead grin.

Suddenly, from out of the blue, this guy started spouting an unsolicited and shameful tirade against the President. "Your boy's getting rolled," muttered the stranger with undisguised glee. As you can probably guess, I run into these goofy Clinton-hating types all the time at my backyard barbecues, so I didn't give it much thought at the time. "Just another hate radio fan," I thought to myself, and returned to my morning cuppa joe.

Now we fast-forward to early August 1994. One day, after my usual afternoon run, I settled into the couch to catch up on my CNN when, under the caption "New Whitewater Independent Counsel," a familiar face stared back at me from the TV. It all came back to me with a jolt—the new independent counsel was the weirdo from the airport!

I'm not big on conspiracy theories, but boy, I can't tell you how suspicious I became when I heard the details of his appointment. I read in the paper the next day that the judge who headed the panel that had removed independent counsel Robert Fiske and appointed Mr. Starr in his place was a Clinton-hater himself. This judge, a North Carolina lawyer named David Sentelle, was a protégé of Senator Jesse Helms, who has publicly threatened the President and is arguably the biggest Clinton-hater in Congress. Sentelle had dropped some of his official ties to the Republican Party when he was appointed to the federal bench. But just as I am a yellow-dog Democrat to the bone, I know that some things about a fella just don't change.

I found it especially interesting that this "former" Republican, Judge Sentelle, was seen having a heated conversation over lunch with Jesse Helms and Lauch Faircloth, North Carolina's terrible two (Republican senators, that is), just before Starr's appointment. Now I'll bet you dollars to doughnuts they weren't talking about finding more funding for Head Start.

Later, I discovered that Judge Sentelle's wife began working for the far-right Senator Faircloth as a low-level staffer five months after Starr's appointment. Now, I'm not Columbo, but even to an LSU dropout like me, this situation didn't add up to anything good.

As you probably know by now from seeing me on TV, I'm an excitable guy. And this whole Starr turn seemed like an injustice beyond belief. I was angrier than I'd been in a long time, so I wrote a letter to the White House, telling them how essential it was to warn the American people about who Ken Starr really was. I also forwarded the letter to the late Ann Devroy, a good friend of mine who wrote for the *Washington Post*. The way I saw it, the American people had chosen a President I had worked long and hard for. And I'd be damned if I would allow Mr. Starr to make partisan use of what was designed to be an impartial office for the purpose of smearing Bill Clinton.

Alas, the powers-that-be at the White House thought an offensive against Starr would be counterproductive, and they begged me to withdraw the letter. Woefully, I gave in to White House pressure. That night, I called Mrs. Devroy at the *Post* and informed her that, in the immortal words of Nixon press secretary Ron Ziegler, the letter was now "inoperative." She was the kind of reporter who kept her word—she was a rare breed. The letter was never published.

Of all the twists, turns, and dead ends this ugly Starr episode has taken since August of 1994, I believe getting talked out of that fight was my personal biggest mistake.

And so, in spite of my adamant beliefs, and the quickly mounting evidence to the contrary, I went along with the accepted White House policy that Kenneth Starr was a man with impeccable motives who could be trusted to search for the truth. Over four long, bad years later, the whole country knows what a bunch of malarkey that is. Looking back at it, that letter I wrote still embodies my true opinion, then as now, of Mr. Starr and his investigation. Here it is.

August 9, 1994

The Honorable Leon Panetta
Chief of Staff
The White House
Washington, D.C. 20500

Dear Mr. Panetta:

I am convinced that the appointment of Kenneth W. Starr as Independent Counsel represents a historic and unconscionable violation of fairness and justice, and that his appointment has been engineered by fanatical opponents of the President and his agenda, who resent Bill Clinton's success in turning our economy around and improving the lives of real Americans in unprecedented fashion.

It is now my intention to speak forthrightly on these issues.

I have previously been constrained from doing so because of my consulting role at the White House and Democratic National Committee. Therefore, I am relinquishing my White House pass (it is enclosed with this

...And the Horse He Rode In On

letter) and have written to the chairman of the DNC, David Wilhelm, asking him to terminate my retainer fee with the Democratic National Committee effective August 1, 1994. I will continue my policy not to lobby on behalf of corporate, special, or foreign interests. I will continue to disclose all relevant personal financial data, as I did on July 15, 1994.

The appointment of Ken Starr, it is now clear, was the result of political pressure from virulent opponents of the President, such as Congressman Dan Burton and Republican political operative Floyd Brown. A partisan judge, one who owes his allegiance to Senator Jesse Helms, has placed Ken Starr, also fiercely partisan, in a position which grants him subpoena power over the President of the United States.

Why? Because the President's opponents have discovered that lies, political assassination, and the grossest partisan manipulation of our legal process I have ever seen can succeed at hiding the President's achievements from the American people.

This decision to relinquish my White House pass and resign from my Democratic National Committee contract was a difficult one, born out of agonizing over this injustice and how ineffectual I feel I have become in defending the President and his achievements. This morning, I saw the wisdom of this decision affirmed in a front-page *Washington Post* headline, "Clinton's Ratings Decline Despite Rising Economy." The story starts off with the observation that "A booming economy has proven to be a political bust for President Clinton . . ." and goes on to express everyone's mystification at the unprecedented disparity between people's perceptions and reality. Well, I'm not mystified. We based the election campaign on a central issue—remember the sign hanging in the War Room—the economy drove that campaign and voter decision making, and the President has delivered *big time*.

However, the band of political hacks, for whom the President and the Administration are an affront and a threat, have hidden these achievements with manipulation after manipulation. Their latest effort is to pressure the federal judiciary to appoint an avowed political enemy of the President to do their bidding.

This is an intolerable situation and I plan on saying it often, speaking only as an individual citizen and not on behalf of the White House or Democratic Party.

Sincerely,

James Carville

As you can see from my letter, I was still mad as hell, and, finally, in October 1996, after hearing that the taxpayer-funded Ken Starr put in an appearance at Pat Robertson's school, I couldn't take it anymore. My mother, Miss Nippy, raised me to be a fighter, and now, embarrassed by my cowardly behavior, I could no longer allow the White House to constrain me to keep quiet about something I knew in my heart was wrong. That's when I began my new

...And the Horse He Rode In On

campaign, the Education and Information Project (EIP), to inform the American people of how unjust and unfair Kenneth Starr's persecution of the President and the First Lady had become.

And man, how the media tore me up for EIP. No surprise, the name-calling started again, and all sorts of malignant motives were attributed to my actions. I showed my letter of August 1994 to some of these detractors. As it illustrates, my motives haven't changed, and my indignation hasn't diminished a bit, since that dark day when Ken Starr was first made independent counsel by a bunch of kooky Clinton-hating conservatives.

Of course, recent events have now validated my position as the first lone voice of dissent against Starr. These many months later, Americans have watched in disbelief as the independent counsel has subpoenaed bookstore owners, lawyers, and mothers in an obsessive attempt to get the President. The good people of this country have heard about Inspector Starr's ties to cigarette companies, Paula Jones's lawyers, and right-wing payola. Every citizen now knows that Whitewater was never anything more than the longest-running political dirty trick in American history, and that Ken Starr's continuing "investigation" is just a partisan witch hunt that goes far beyond the bounds of anything Congress ever had in mind when it created the independent counsel statute.

This book will lay out the case against Mr. Starr's investigation. There's been more hot air than usual blowing in Washington these last couple of months about this mess. It's enough to make you dizzy. But what I'm gonna do is take apart Mr. Starr's octopus of an investigation point by point and show you that it's little more than a sham. It ain't always easy to understand, because there are just so many instances of manipulation, orchestration, and back-scratching, but it will become clear that, like the good First Lady warned us, there is something of a conspiracy afoot. But I promise to go nice and smooth, so by the end you'll know the absolute facts as well as most of the so-called experts and television pundits who make a living jabbering about this trumped-up pile of nothing.

Chances are, if you've bought this book, you don't like Ken Starr either. And I have to warn you, once we get through the smoke and reveal the truth, and see just how out of control Mr. Starr has become, you're going to be as mad, upset, and outraged as this here ragin' Cajun.

He Crawled from the Deep:

Ken Starr and Whitewater

As with mosquitoes, horseflies, and most bloodsucking parasites, Kenneth Starr was spawned in stagnant water.

The independent counsel first emerged on the national scene in 1994 to investigate Whitewater, a failed Arkansas land deal that dated from 1978 in which the President and the First Lady had the misfortune to lose an investment of $42,000. With the craven aid of a tightly knit gang of right-wing operatives, Ken Starr came forth like the Creature from the Black Lagoon, hell-bent on terrorizing the inhabitants of Little Rock in a single-minded quest to defame the President of the United States.

And so before we look at Starr's more recent deceptions, intimidations, and screwups, it's important to revisit this old Arkansas haunt for a spell. Like me, most of you have heard so much mind-numbing blather about Whitewater, the last thing in the world you want to do is take a trip back there. But bear with me here, because the origins of the Whitewater scam shed light not only on the early stages of the anti-Clinton media madness, but also on the independent counsel's countless conflicts of interest since the first days of his appointment. Over four years and $40 million after he first started peeking under stones in Little Rock, the only thing Ken Starr ever exposed was himself: the fact that his investigation was an absolutely baseless, politically contrived, right-wing-backed, taxpayer-subsidized smear campaign from the get-go.

* * *

According to the original article that let the monkey out of the cage (written by Jeff Gerth for the *New York Times* in 1992 and widely promulgated since by the *Times*, the *Washington Post*, and other purported bastions of national journalism), the Whitewater story goes a little something like this: In 1978, the Clintons, along with old friends Jim and Susan McDougal, invested some money in a real estate deal in the Ozark Mountains. When it turned out that the McDougals had no capital, then Governor Clinton may or may not have helped to secure a $300,000 loan for his business associates so they could attract more investors to the land deal, which, along with that original loan, eventually tanked.

Some have speculated—wrongly—that $50,000 of this bad loan went toward covering the Clintons' interests in Whitewater. Further baseless speculation claimed that Hillary Clinton, then an attorney for the Rose Law Firm, may have cooked the books on the Whitewater deal in order to cover up any evidence of Clintonian wrongdoing regarding that loan. Of course, there never was, nor has there ever been, any evidence of malfeasance by either the President or the First Lady. But that didn't stop the scandal-hungry media and Clinton-hating Republicans from crazy-legging for the end zone with the fable.

Sometime after Gerth's confused and confusing 1992 newspaper piece, the national press went into full-froth mode. While the Sunday morning pundits professed their shock and indignation for the television cameras, every major newspaper, magazine, and news program in the country sent its crack journalists to Little Rock to uncover the "truth" about a busted twenty-year-old land deal. It wasn't too long before publications across the country were jam-packed with badly reasoned, badly written stories by Bob Woodward wannabes, each one trying desperately to inject some life into an absurd heap of baseless, nonsensical allegations.

Woodward on Whitewater

While most of the media community has tried every which way to make a Watergate out of Whitewater, journalistic legend Bob Woodward sees the Whitewater investigation in a completely different light. When Woodward was asked to compare the two investigations on *Larry King Live*, the man who brought down Nixon had this to say about the allegations against President Clinton:

"No, [Whitewater is not like Watergate], because there are no tapes. There are no witnesses that are really credible, who are contemporaneous, to say 'I was there, and Clinton said, let's do this that's illegal, or let's do this that's corrupt.' And we have years of inquiries, and you have to think as a reporter on all of these things, you know, maybe he didn't do any of them.

"There are kinds of allegations that shoot all over the place all of the time, and no one is a greater repository of allegations than Bill Clinton. And no doubt some of them, or maybe lots of them, are false—or maybe even all of them are false.

"But the things linger. There's no closure. All of the Clinton scandals, if you look at them, they've piled up. They're like airplanes circling National Airport, and none have landed."[1]

For example, check out this howler penned by columnist Michael Kramer for *Time* magazine (and later dissected by Gene Lyons in his book *Fools for Scandal: How the Media Invented Whitewater*):

"[Whitewater is] different—*or could be*—because the wrongdoing *(if there was any) may have involved* abuses of power while Clinton was serving as Governor of Arkansas. On the other hand, Whitewater too is from the past. So *even if* the worst were proved—and *no one yet knows what that is*—the offense *might not* warrant impeachment [italics Lyons's]."[2]

Hmmm . . . With all that crazy logic, all those ifs, mights, maybes, and could bes, it sounds like something that might've been written by *Seinfeld*'s Kramer instead of *Time*'s Kramer. Back when I was a student at LSU Law School, we had a saying: If "ifs" and "buts" were beer and nuts, we'd have ourselves a heck of a party. Nevertheless, wrongheaded reporters like Michael Kramer weren't the only ones to lose their minds over Arkansas real estate. Still nursing their wounds from the 1992 presidential election, the fringe right was champing at the bit to find anything, real or imaginary, that could take down America's new President.

When conservatives caught wind of Whitewater, they flocked to the rumors like Newt Gingrich to a plate of hot pork chops. Faster than you can say "media hype," the GOP was hollering louder than a stuck pig. Rush Limbaugh, Jerry Falwell, and Pat Robertson spun the yarn endlessly to their sycophantic audiences, while Senator Alfonse D'Amato, never one to miss a chance for free publicity at someone else's expense, initiated congressional hearings in order to have his face plastered all over C-SPAN.

With the knee-jerk help of the editorial departments of the scandal-hungry national press, the GOP soon raised such a racket that the able, conscientious, and long-suffering U.S. attorney general, Janet Reno, was politically compelled to appoint an independent counsel.

When Reno settled on Republican attorney Robert Fiske to look into Whitewater, there was a lot of rejoicing among conservatives. Senator Bob Dole remarked that "people who know him think he is extremely well-qualified [and] independent."[3] Self-styled Whitewater conspiracy theorist Al D'Amato gushed that Fiske was "one of the most honorable and skilled lawyers." (It should be noted that D'Amato received $3,000 in campaign donations from Mr. Fiske.) "He is a man of enormous integrity," remarked the Republican senator from New York. "He's fine, he's talented, he is a man of great loyalty."[4]

Unfortunately for the country at large, the fringe right was not so pleased with the credentials of Mr. Fiske. These folks, having gone to the considerable trouble of contriving and publicizing bogus criminal acts related to the Whitewater deal, hated seeing *any* independent counsel appointed (no matter that he was a good GOP member) who might discover how insignificant the whole episode truly was. Although Mr. Fiske had contributed several thousand dollars to Republican candidates and committees over the years, he still wasn't partisan enough to satisfy the wacko right.[5] What the anti-Clinton crazies wanted was a real old-school hatchet man. And there was no one more qualified to dig one up than Jesse Helms.

Take Your Toys and Go Home

Although the cries for Robert Fiske's removal came most loudly and hysterically from the far right, a few national newspapers also joined in this caterwauling chorus. *The Wall Street Journal,* in particular, painted Fiske as Public Enemy No. 1. The *Journal*'s editorial page attacked Fiske's decision to quit his private practice and called his investigation a "cover-up" and an attempt at "political damage control."

Why such a bloodthirsty attack from such a respected broadsheet? Well, in his report to Congress on the suicide of White House counsel Vincent Foster, Fiske had numbered among the reasons for Foster's tragic death the many "mean-spirited and factually baseless" editorials of *The Wall Street Journal.* Apparently for the obstinate, conspiracy-minded editorial department of the *Journal*, two wrongs, no matter how downright shabby or horrific their consequences, still make a right.[6]

Helms and Lauch Faircloth, the unofficial spokesmen for the raving ultraright, paid a visit to a fellow Tarheel, Judge David Sentelle. But they weren't just paying a call on a neighbor for some iced tea. Helms and Faircloth don't go anywhere without a program, and they had one to share with Judge Sentelle. Judge Sentelle, by fortuitous coincidence, was head of a three-judge panel that oversees the independent counsel. And by an equally happy coincidence, Sentelle happened to have a cozy history with Senator Helms.

Not only is the good judge a member of Helms's conservative National Congressional Club and a longtime Helms supporter, but his very appointment to the federal bench was sponsored by none other than that esteemed senior senator from North Carolina.[7] Heck, he even served on the appeals panel that overturned the conviction of that old renegade colonel and Iran-contra operative Oliver North.

How Helms Is He?

Make no mistake about it: When I say David Sentelle is an ultraconservative Helmsman, I ain't just whistling Dixie. For one thing, he served as the chair of the Mecklenburg County (Charlotte, North Carolina) Republican Party. Moreover, according to *Rolling*

Stone magazine, not only did Sentelle refuse to resign his membership at some white-only private clubs during his confirmation hearing, he also penned the following words about country music for a 1981 book entitled *Why the South Will Survive*: "The main appeal of the music of the South is found among . . . the long-historied, little-loved descendants of the people who built half the civilized world—the Anglo-Saxons."[8]

And as if Kenneth Starr weren't enough of an attack on the President, David Sentelle and his cronies have appointed at least three other independent counsels in their apparent attempt to stymie the progress of the Clinton administration.

* * *

Now to this day nobody really knows what those three men discussed at their table. Sentelle declared that they spoke about cowboy gear and their prostates (a great lunchtime topic if you don't feel like eating much). But you've got to ask yourself, as I did, if it's possible that maybe, just maybe, North Carolina's dynamic Clinton-bashing duo put in a request for a more aggressive partisan prosecutor, one who would work harder to make a Niagara Falls out of Whitewater.

Well, all I know is what happened after that lunch: Less than a month later—just eight months after Robert Fiske had been appointed as independent counsel—Judge Sentelle suddenly fired Mr. Fiske for "perceptions of conflict" mainly arising from his having been appointed by Janet Reno. And then his wife got a nice job working for Senator Faircloth not too long after.

And by now, you know who Judge Sentelle's panel appointed in Fiske's place.

That Old Airport Clinton-Basher, Kenneth Starr.

Good people, I'll give it to you short and sweet. In the history of the independent counsel statute, there has never been a prosecutor appointed who's as fiercely partisan as Kenneth Starr.

That bears some repeating: Never In History.

It'd be one thing if the guy had gone to a few Republican rallies in his time, or had once argued a case adverse to the Clinton administration. But this was ridiculous. Between his private practice, his prior casework, and his ties to the GOP right wing, Ken Starr had more conflicts than a John Grisham novel.

In a recent, well-publicized interview, the now infamous independent counsel compared himself to Jack Webb of *Dragnet*, claiming he was interested in "Just the facts, ma'am." Well, Ken Starr ain't the only *Dragnet* fan in these parts. So, with a tip of the hat to Joe Friday, I reassembled the old Carville Rapid Response Team to see what they could find in the public record about Ken Starr.

Let me tell you, it didn't take very long before they uncovered quite a few unappealing facts about the appointment and tenure of our inglorious independent persecutor:

 FACT   *Ken Starr was appointed by a panel headed by right-wing judge David Sentelle just after Sentelle's lunch meeting with ultraconservative North Carolina senators Jesse Helms and Lauch Faircloth.*

I've already talked about this outrage myself, so let's hear what some other folks had to say about the results of that mystery meal.

At the time of Inspector Starr's appointment, *five* former presidents of the American Bar Association, in a letter that questioned the three-judge panel's impartiality, criticized Judge Sentelle's conduct. Stephen Bundy, a prominent University of California, Berkeley, law professor, had this to say about Sentelle's ruse: "The whole point of giving [the case] to judges is that they will be immune from political influence. . . . Why else would they feel compelled to review Reno's judgment except that she is presumed to be politically influenced and he is not? Then we find this guy consorting with the leader of the opposing political faction. . . . At best it appears to be improper."[9]

FACT *Ken Starr was extremely active in Republican politics.*

Unlike his predecessor, Robert Fiske (who had donated only money to campaigns), Starr also devoted a lot of his time and energy to the Grand Old Party before he was called on to become a so-called independent counsel. Starr co-chaired the unsuccessful 1994 congressional campaign of Republican Kyle McSlarrow, now the campaign manager for former vice president Dan Quayle, against Democrat Jim Moran. (It says a lot about Starr's professional skills that he was one of the few folks around who couldn't get a Republican congressional candidate elected in 1994.) Moreover, Mr. Starr even contemplated running for the Virginia Senate as a Republican in 1993, but I guess he figured he could do more damage to the Democrats (and the country) in other ways.

Finally, Ken Starr also did put his money where his mouth was. He contributed $5,475 to the campaigns of six Republican political candidates in the 1993–94 election cycle. Then, *while serving as independent counsel,* he gave an additional $1,750 to a political action committee (PAC) that supported several 1996 GOP presidential campaigns, including those of Phil Gramm, Richard Lugar, Lamar Alexander, and Bob Dole.[10]

Isn't it funny how the press jumped all over journalist Steven Brill for donating money to the Democrats, but you hardly ever hear mention of the Republican donations of a man with subpoena power?

Ken Starr:
Right-Wing Party Animal

To no one's surprise, Ken Starr also found time in his busy schedule as Whitewater counsel to become a fixture on the right-wing party scene, and a GOP attack dog. Check out this story by reformed Clinton antagonist David Brock:

"I had been a guest at the wedding of Barbara and Ted Olson, the Washington super-lawyer who counts President Reagan and *The American Spectator,* the magazine where I work, among his clients. *On hand was the entire anti-Clinton establishment,* everyone from *Wall Street Journal* editorial-page editor Robert Bartley to *Whitewater independent counsel Kenneth Starr. . . .* Former Bush White House counsel C. Boyden Gray joked that *since it looked as if Kenneth Starr was not going to come up with the goods before the election,* it was up to me to derail the Clinton juggernaut [my italics]."[11]

FACT   *Ken Starr wrote friend-of-the-court briefs for both pro-GOP and anti-Clinton cases.*

On top of sending in his checks, Ken Starr certainly knew how to feed the GOP bulldog: The good judge also made the great effort to show his anti-Clinton bias through his professional favors. Starr once penned a friend-of-the-court brief on behalf of the Republican National Committee, in a case involving Bush attorney general Richard Thornburgh. And before the American taxpayer began footing the bill for his Whitewater work, Starr decided to take on some pro bono work on behalf of Paula Jones, composing a pro-Paula friend-of-the-court brief for the Supreme Court. Miraculously, the habitually clueless Inspector did sense a conflict of interest here, and at the last minute chose not to submit his *amicus* brief. He's also done work for an organization funded by his billionaire hard-right friend Richard Scaife—the so-called Independent Women's Forum.[12]

In fact, the Ken Starr and Paula Jones camps have intermingled an awful lot. But we'll get to those travesties in good time.

...And the Horse He Rode In On

FACT *Ken Starr represented tobacco companies in his private practice while serving as independent counsel.*

Now let me see if I have this straight: Kenneth Starr oversees a huge staff of lawyers and FBI agents who jet around the country subpoenaing people. He has slavered over his sex-obsessed investigation for over four years and spent more than 40 million taxpayer dollars to finance his fixation. It would seem like he's a pretty busy guy.

Isn't it funny that he still hasn't quit his day job?

Unlike many of his predecessors, including Robert Fiske, Ken Starr chose to continue his million-dollar-a-year private practice at the law firm of Kirkland & Ellis after his appointment as independent counsel. As if he weren't compromised enough already, this decision by Judge Starr created several more appalling, insurmountable conflicts of interest for his investigation.

First among those are Starr's ties to the tobacco industry. As it turns out, Mr. Starr has been working simultaneously as independent counsel and as a cigarette lawyer, representing Brown & Williamson and Philip Morris in a 1996 class-action lawsuit.

So while our President led a valiant campaign to reduce teenage smoking and prevent cigarette companies from selling their dangerous products to our kids (and, I might add, while Bob Dole was telling people tobacco isn't addictive), Bill Clinton was being investigated at every turn by a man cashing checks from Joe Camel and the Marlboro Man![13]

(To be fair, Ken Starr has more than just sex and cigarettes on the brain. When asked to provide a roster of Starr's clients in 1994 and 1995, his lawyer Terry Adamson cited a list that includes the American Automobile Manufacturing Association; Apple Computer; Bell Atlantic; Brown & Williamson Tobacco; Citisteel; General Motors; Ray Hays; G. Stokely; Hughes Aircraft; Victor Posner; Suzuki Motors; the Newspaper Association of America; Philip Morris; Quaker Oats; the Select Committee on Ethics; Southwestern Bell; United Airlines; United Technologies; Allied Signal; Amoco; and the Bradley Foundation.)[14]

Finally, after four years as the independent persecutor, Ken Starr parted company with Kirkland & Ellis. Whether Kirkland & Ellis had the good sense to let him go or whether he needed more time to focus on sex, we don't know.

FACT *Ken Starr's law firm, Kirkland & Ellis, was being sued by the Resolution Trust Corporation, a group that Starr investigated.*

Nineteen months after Ken Starr took the job as independent counsel, yet another conflict came to light. One of the many groups Starr investigated in his role as Whitewater prosecutor was the Resolution Trust Corporation (RTC), a government agency in charge of liquidating failed savings and loans.

What does the RTC have to do with Whitewater? Well, it was an RTC senior investigator named L. Jean Lewis who began an inquiry into the Whitewater deal in the first place.

...And the Horse He Rode In On

L. Jean Lewis

In his darker moments Ken Starr probably looks to the patron saint of Whitewater, L. Jean Lewis, for inspiration. She was a true pioneer and visionary for his never-ending Clinton-hating campaign.

As a Resolution Trust Corporation investigator in Kansas City, L. Jean Lewis obsessively pursued a criminal case against officials of Madison Guaranty Savings & Loan. As my friends in the War Room (the Little Rock headquarters for the Clinton presidential campaign in 1992) and I were getting the good word out about then Governor Clinton, L. Jean Lewis was busy scratching up scandal. As she reportedly told New York senator Alfonse D'Amato, she had set a deadline of August 31, 1992, for the results of her grubby work. (This would give her just enough time to have an impact on the November election with her revelations.) She also told Little Rock FBI agent Steve Irons that her goal was to change the course of history. She was two days late.

On September 2, 1992, she sent a criminal referral to the U.S. attorney in Little Rock that named the President and the First Lady as possible witnesses to and beneficiaries of criminal wrongdoing. She hounded the attorney general and FBI agents about the referral. But the Justice Department felt there was no real case against the Clintons and, to their eternal credit, history has proven them correct.

But the story of L. Jean Lewis would get even more pitiful: Two years later the would-be whistle-blower and RTC investigator was being investigated herself by the RTC for a variety of alleged abuses, including improper disclosure of confidential documents; secretly taping RTC employees; keeping confidential documents at home; and use of government equipment for personal gain. Lewis admitted that she used her office to market T-shirts and coffee mugs lettered "B.I.T.C.H." ("Bubba, I'm Taking Charge, Hillary.")[15]

Sounds like a pretty impartial and reliable investigator, doesn't she?

After L. Jean Lewis was suspended from the investigation, Starr, true to form, quickly began scrutinizing the RTC to uncover why L. Jean Lewis had been taken off the case.

You might ask, so what? It doesn't seem that big a deal, and Ken Starr might just be a curious guy. But nothing's ever that simple when you're dealing with the Inspector.

It just so happens that while Starr was scrutinizing the RTC for allegedly covering up Whitewater, the RTC was itself suing Starr's private practice for aiding and abetting breaches of fiduciary responsibility. In other words, Starr was investigating the RTC for its connections to a bad loan (the $300,000 Whitewater loan) at the same time that the RTC was suing Starr's firm for *its* connections to a failed savings and loan. In fact, Ken Starr subpoenaed the *very same people* for his case who were involved in the lawsuit against Kirkland & Ellis! So you tell me: Was Ken Starr dispassionately serving the public interest with his inquiry into the RTC, or was he, by twisting the arms of those who threatened to expose its wrongdoing, serving the interests of the law firm that has made him wealthy?

Interesting question.

And how does our esteemed independent counsel respond? Well, despite the fact that Starr was a senior partner at Kirkland & Ellis and served on his firm's management committee, he claims he knew nothing of the RTC lawsuit against Kirkland & Ellis until October of 1995, *more than two and a half years* after the RTC filed it. Wake up, Ken: You're not paying attention in those management meetings.

Whatever the case, the RTC and Kirkland & Ellis reached a confidential settlement in 1996. Yet, the question remains: Why was this particular conflict of interest not disclosed by either Starr *or* the two Republican-led congressional committees overseeing his work? Inquiring minds want to know.[16]

 FACT *Ken Starr represented International Paper, the company that sold land (and lost money on it) to the Whitewater Development Company.*

Yes, folks, the hits just keep on coming. When Ken Starr took the position of independent counsel, he was also representing International Paper. This particular conflict is made even more damning by the fact that critics of Robert Fiske (Ken Starr's predecessor) had claimed that *his* independence was compromised because his firm—Davis, Polk & Wardwell—had also represented International Paper. Ironic, isn't it, that Fiske severed all ties with his firm upon his appointment as independent counsel, while

Ken Starr happily continued raking in the dough from his private practice?[17]

FACT *Ken Starr is a member of and has worked for several prominent conservative groups.*

Besides his ties to the Republican Party, Ken Starr is a member of more right-wing organizations than you can shake a stick at. The Inspector is a member of the Washington Legal Foundation, a conservative lawyers group funded in part by the tobacco industry, and the Federalist Club, a prominent Washington organization of conservative lawyers. Moreover, Starr has done paid legal work for the Bradley Organization, a Richard Scaife–funded outfit that also supports the Landmark Legal Foundation, the Free Congress Foundation, and *The American Spectator* magazine, all renowned anti-Clinton groups. Starr's predecessor had been vilified by the right for his ties to some liberal organizations, but, as with the International Paper episode, Starr's own ties to conservative groups are seen, amazingly, to have no bearing on this man's impartiality.

FACT *Ken Starr made speeches to anti–Clinton organizations while serving as independent counsel.*

As if he didn't have enough conflicts of interest from the get-go, Starr somehow managed to stumble into a few more during the course of his investigation. When the Whitewater counsel wasn't probing into people's private sexual histories or harassing the citizens of Little Rock, he was speaking at various conservative get-togethers, including a speech for another Scaife-funded organization, a property rights group, and a talk, in October 1996, at televangelist Pat Robertson's Regent University. Of the latter, Starr's friend and colleague Joseph diGenova remarked, "I probably would not have gone and talked to Pat Robertson's people at a time when you give people like James Carville a perfectly nice target to take a shot at."[18]

Mr. diGenova, you have a point.

FACT   *Ken Starr flirted with a deanship at Pepperdine University, a post funded by right-wing godfather Richard Mellon Scaife.*

Maybe he was sick and tired of his phony investigation. Maybe he unaccountably felt a glimmer of conscience. Maybe he listened to too many Beach Boys songs. But whatever the reason, in February of 1997 "Hang Ten" Ken announced—or, more to the point, his aides announced—that the independent counsel was giving it up and heading for the beach.

Specifically, Ken Starr accepted a job as the dean of Pepperdine University's Schools of Law and Public Policy, which has received substantial contributions from Richard Scaife, the man *Time* magazine called "the premier sugar daddy of the American right."[19] Only after tremendous public pressure from the scandal-loving editorial departments of the *New York Times* and *Washington Post*, and from such conservative luminaries as columnist William Safire and ad man Floyd Brown, did Starr decide to postpone his Malibu move until he "completed" his role as independent persecutor.

FACT *Ken Starr was forced by Associate Attorney General Webster Hubbell to stop representing Bell Atlantic.*

Why has Webb Hubbell been so badly victimized by Ken Starr during the past four years? That's one of the easy questions to answer. As it turns out, a 1993 case involving Bell Atlantic made a strong connection to the origins of the independent counsel's rancor.

During Starr's final days as solicitor general of the Bush administration, Bell Atlantic sued the federal government in an attempt to overturn a ban on phone companies becoming involved in providing video services (a ban that was later overturned during the Clinton administration). Though it has long been thought a conflict of interest for a lawyer to take a case against the government that arose while that lawyer was working for the government, private citizen Starr, never one to pass up a deal that might increase his bank account or get him some attention, signed on with the Bell Atlantic legal team in 1993. Much to Starr's annoyance, then

Associate Attorney General Webster Hubbell informed him that the Justice Department was concerned that a conflict of interest existed and that, legally, he might not be able to take the case.[20]

And as poor Webb Hubbell learned the hard way, you don't want to get between Ken Starr and someone else's money.

During the Whitewater mess, Starr raked Hubbell over the coals but good. Hubbell probably could have gotten off a lot easier if he'd been willing to lie about the President, but he's an honorable man. He held firm. "The office of independent counsel can indict my dog," he said. "They can indict my cat, but I'm not going to lie about the President. I'm not going to lie about the First Lady."

Heck, if Ken Starr could have figured out a way to get a dog to hold his paw over a Bible, I guarantee he would have subpoenaed that hound and the litter he came from.

Fortunately, a federal judge has come forward to liberate Hubbell from the wrath of Starr and put a stop to the Inspector's sordid abuse of American law. Calling the independent counsel's case against Hubbell "a quintessential fishing expedition" and his tactics "scary," a federal judge threw Starr's attempts to destroy Webb Hubbell out of court and into the gutter where they belonged.[21]

Starr's Predecessors Speak Out

Look, folks, I'm not the only guy out here who thinks Ken Starr's conflicts of interest are reprehensible, irreconcilable, and just plain irresponsible. Here's what some former independent counsels had to say about this new breed of persecuting prosecutor:

Gerald Gallinghouse (a Republican who investigated a drug allegation in the Jimmy Carter administration):

Starr is "devoting a hell of a lot of time to private practice. He should get in or get out. I don't give a damn about the Republicans, Democrats, Bull Moose, or mugwumps. He should get on with the investigation and bring it to a conclusion as soon as practicable. And you're not going to do it with the top man running all over the country making speeches and taking care of private clients."

Lawrence Walsh (Iran-contra independent counsel):

"The one excuse [for employing] an independent counsel is his independence. If not necessarily full-time detachment from everything else, he [at least] can't be involved with anything that impairs his freedom of action."

Whitney North Seymour Jr. (got the conviction of Reagan aide Michael Deaver for perjury):

"When we were engaged in the intensive parts of the investigation or trial preparation, I did not have time for anything else."

James C. McKay (investigated Reagan aide Lyn Nofziger):

"I shed everything [else] I was doing after a month. I was devoting 99.9 percent of my time to the job I was given to do. I felt like I could concentrate on the very difficult problems much better if I did that, and the job could be done more quickly."[22]

40+ Million Dollars Goes a Long Way

On November 19, 1997, the *Washington Post* tallied the cost of the FBI investigation into the tragedy of TWA Flight 800. According to the *Post*, "Investigators spent 16 months on the crash investigation, during which the FBI conducted more than 7,000 interviews, pursued over 3,000 public leads, and took 2,000 chemical swabs from parts of the wreckage to look for traces of explosives. Every piece of cargo aboard the flight was traced from its point of origin to the jet's cargo holds, and every worker who touched the plane and anything that went into it—including the on-board movies— was examined." The cost of this exhaustive study was between *$14 and $20 million*.

In contrast, at last accounting Starr has spent four years and *$40 million* on his Whitewater investigation, with absolutely nothing to show for it. To put things in perspective, Ken Starr has spent twice as much looking into a lousy land deal that lost $40,000 than the FBI spent conclusively proving the cause of a crash that killed 230 people.

Where the heck did all this money go? Am I the only man in Washington sane enough (or crazy enough) to think we've horrendously misplaced priorities?

Here are the costs of some recent federal investigations, all of which came to significant conclusions—except Whitewater.

FBI investigation into the 1993
World Trade Center bombing
(resulted in successful convictions) $9.9 million

FBI investigation into the crash
of TWA Flight 800 (determined
no criminal act involved) $17 million (est.)

"Independent" counsel Kenneth Starr's
Whitewater investigation
(no evidence found of the
Clintons' involvement) $40 million (est.)

Total cost of Whitewater investigations
(no evidence found of
the Clintons' involvement) $51.4 million (est.)

Eighteen-year-long investigation and
manhunt for the Unabomber
(suspect apprehended and convicted) $50 million

40+ Million Dollars Goes a Long Way, Part II

Cost to date of Ken Starr's
Whitewater investigation $40 million

Number of additional police officers under the
COPS program that could be financed for a year
by the cost of Starr's investigation 1,544

Number of officers on selected
major city police forces

Seattle:	1,238
Kansas City:	1,179
Nashville:	1,166
Fort Worth:	1,166
Pittsburgh:	1,148
Miami:	1,027
Indianapolis:	1,013

Number of teachers that could be
financed for a year by the cost of
Starr's investigation[23] 1,142

Ken Starr's Critical Conditions

So, if you're like me, you're probably wondering how Ken Starr managed to drag out the Whitewater investigation for so long without anyone getting wise to him. His secret: Whet the appetites of lazy reporters with talk of "critical stages." Check out how many times Mr. Starr has come close to the big breakthrough:

August 18, 1995: The indictment of the McDougals signifies that "Starr's 18-month-long investigation . . . has reached a critical phase." (*Washington Post*)

August 23, 1995: The First Lady's Whitewater testimony "is a strong indication that his widening inquiry has reached a critical new phase." (*New York Times*)

September 12, 1995: Former segregationist and lead Clinton-hater Jim Johnson announces that "the Whitewater investigation moves into its most critical stage." (*Washington Times*)

October 12, 1995: Ken Starr writes a letter to the Senate Whitewater Committee claiming his investigation has reached a critical stage. (*Arkansas Democrat-Gazette*)

May 29, 1996: Guilty verdicts for the McDougals "may mark the opening of a new phase in Whitewater." (*Washington Post*)

October 4, 1996: Ken Starr announces in his Pat Robertson speech that his investigation is in "an important phase." (*Memphis Commercial Appeal*)

November 7, 1996: As Bill Clinton wins a second term, "the independent counsel investigation of his Whitewater real estate investment approaches a critical stage." (*Washington Post*)

November 13, 1996: Ken Starr tells an audience at the Detroit Economic Club that his "investigation is at a critical juncture now, and we are proceeding as expeditiously as possible." (*Wall Street Journal*)

December 2, 1996: Newsweek reports that the Whitewater probe "is at a critical stage. 'We are very far along,' Starr says." (*Newsweek*)

February 23, 1997: Ken Starr decides to forgo Pepperdine University and return to his investigation, claiming his investigation has reached a critical phase. (*Chicago Sun-Times*)

April 27, 1997: Ken Starr's Little Rock grand jury is extended six months, marking a "new and potentially damaging phase." (*Richmond Times-Dispatch*)

January 5, 1998: The *Washington Post* runs a Sue Schmidt article with the headline "Pressure for Testimony Rises as Whitewater Probe Nears Crucial Phase." According to the lead paragraph, the investigation is now reaching a "critical juncture." (*Washington Post*)

Sheesh . . . I've never seen anything in critical condition that long without being declared dead halfway through. At this point in this ugly game, the only things to be critical of are Ken Starr's odious and protracted investigation and all the reporters out there who don't know how to use a thesaurus!

Getting It Wrong on Whitewater

Of all the nuances of the convoluted Whitewater story, the one that seemed most damning to the President and First Lady was the allegation that $50,000 of the bad $300,000 loan went to help Whitewater. If that were fact, as various irrational Clinton-haters in the press have opined, it would mean the Clintons had taken money from the government and used it to line their own pockets.

Sadly for all these outraged reporters, it doesn't come close to the truth. As Professor Gilbert Cranberg of the University of Iowa School of Journalism noted in an article for the *Nieman Reports*, the tale of the $50,000 is a "key element" of Whitewater "that's been written about carelessly, or incompletely, or just plain falsely."

...And the Horse He Rode In On

In sum, Cranberg remarks, any decent journalist could tell you that this story is nothing more than a $50,000 lie.

Cranberg notes that the $50,000 that's referred to was comprised of two "chunks, one for $24,455 and one for $25,000." Chunk 1 ($24,455), part of a 1985 loan to James McDougal from the Stephens Security Bank, was placed in the Whitewater account a full year *before* David Hale's bum loan, and was in fact repaid by McDougal before the Hale loan even took place! Chunk 2 ($25,000), used by James McDougal to buy land near the Whitewater project in 1986, was never actually in the Whitewater account, and in fact "messed up Whitewater's balance sheet . . . adding a huge liability."

In short, half of this money that the Clintons were accused of stealing from the government had absolutely nothing to do with them or the infamous bad loan, and the other half was used by James McDougal for a separate deal and ended up *losing* money for the Clintons![24]

So much for *that* outrage. I guess it's probably too much to demand an apology from all the shoddy journalists who were quick to publicly lambaste the President and First Lady before they checked their reporting.

Fools for Scandal: The Real Story of Whitewater

Aspiring journalists take note: While the rest of the national media were falling over themselves to publish nonsensical stories about imaginary misdeeds, one reporter from the *Arkansas Democrat-Gazette*, Gene Lyons, chose to break ranks and investigate the real scandal about Whitewater—the failure of almost everyone in the national press to even attempt a coherent understanding of what really happened. Lyons's book, *Fools for Scandal*, is hands down the best read you're going to find about the Whitewater scandal. Since the book exposes the complete idiocy of the journalistic establishment over this issue, naturally it was panned in the *New York Times* as a "nasty" book.[25] Nevertheless, to those of you who want to pierce the veil of deceit and find out how seriously screwed up today's reporting can be, I highly recommend it.

Follow the Money:

Whitewater and Right-Wing Payola

Good news! After four long years and millions upon millions of taxpayer dollars, some evidence of criminal behavior related to Whitewater has *finally* been uncovered. But, sadly for Ken Starr, it turns out that it may be *his investigation that's committed the crime.*

Thanks to *Salon* magazine and the *New York Observer*, which both hunkered down and did some real reporting, abandoning the prevailing media precedent of printing scurrilous leaks spoon-fed from Starr's office, the very foundation of Starr's judicial probe has now been exposed for what it is: a political dirty trick shot through with clandestine encounters and right-wing kickbacks. You see, as it happens, David Hale, the independent counsel's star Whitewater witness and a man Judge Starr has publicly declared to be utterly truthful, may have been on the right-wing payroll from the beginning.

That's right, folks, at the same time David Hale, as official court jester, was implicating the President and First Lady for Ken Starr's perpetual amusement, he may have been getting cash from the adversaries of the President, including Starr's own original cash cow, Richard Mellon Scaife.

Even more intriguing, some suggest that *Starr himself* may have known about the payoffs to Hale. (Starr denies it.) Now it's the investigator who must be investigated, both his motives and his competence. As you'll read below, Starr's four-year fishing expedition actually started out in the belly of an Arkansas bait shop. And it looks like the independent counsel might have gotten caught on his own hook.

Birth of the Right-Wing Conspiracy: The Arkansas Project

In reality, the origins of the Whitewater smear campaign have nothing to do with the actual land deal from whence it took its name. Rather, like many of the fringe right operations in America today, this travesty of an investigation blossomed from the well-lined pockets of Richard Mellon Scaife.

First a few words about this Richard Mellon

Scaife, the archconservative godfather in this heavily funded war against the President. He's the sixty-four-year-old billionaire scion of the Mellon banking family. He's sometimes called a publisher because he owns the *Pittsburgh Tribune-Review*.

He once gave $1 million to Richard Nixon's 1972 campaign and he's still got plenty more where that came from: Scaife has supported the right-wing magazine *The American Spectator*, Starr's seat at Pepperdine University, the Landmark Legal Foundation, and ex-FBI agent Gary Aldrich's lousy, Clinton-hating memoir, and even underwritten some of Paula Jones's and Matt Drudge's legal fees.[1]

After the American people elected Bill Clinton in 1992, Scaife seems to have decided to use his inherited stockpile to upend the democratic process and bring down the new President. He gave $1.7 million of *tax-exempt* money to several ostensibly "charitable" foundations that financed a surreptitious campaign known as the Arkansas Project. Run out of the offices of *The American Spectator* (which is edited by primo Clinton-hater R. Emmett Tyrrell), the Arkansas Project aimed to discredit the President and First Lady by digging up dirt from their time in the governor's mansion.

The Scaife money eventually ended up in the hands of a Mr. Stephen S. Boynton, a longtime conservative activist, who then reportedly used it to pay investigators to "discover" any dirty laundry left behind in Arkansas by the President and First Lady.

One of the men feeding information to Boynton from the Arkansas Project account was a fellow named Parker Dozhier, the owner of a bait shop in Hot Springs, Arkansas. According to

Dozhier, he was paid around $35,000 to gather information on Whitewater, such as newspaper and magazine clippings, for *The American Spectator*. Dozhier does not explain how he fell into this simpleminded, overpaying gig, nor does he ever reveal why the editors of the *Spectator* would happen to choose a worm salesman to serve their research needs. Must've been something about his hands always being in the dirt.

However, others shed more light on the true nature of Dozhier's strange employment. According to both Caryn Mann, Dozhier's live-in girlfriend of several years, and her son, Joshua Rand, who is now a seventeen-year-old student at the University of Arkansas, Parker Dozhier was actually paid a heap of money from the Arkansas Project. Even more alarming is the fact that, according to Ms. Mann's son, at least $5,000 of this ill-gotten tax-exempt loot was handed over in cash payments to Whitewater witness David Hale.

Now just who exactly *is* David Hale? you might ask. Well, to put it simply, he's the only person in the entire Whitewater investigation to claim that the President was aware of, and involved in the procurement of, the $300,000 loan at the heart of this long-running hoax. As such, he happens to be Starr's star witness (in fact, he's pretty much the independent counsel's only witness), and, by all standards of legality and propriety, should be the last man in the world receiving right-wing kickbacks.

Well, unhappily for the suffering American legal system, that doesn't seem to be the way of it. "Parker [Dozhier] would receive money from Boynton," recalls young Joshua Rand. He "would essentially put that in his right pocket, and then he'd pull money out of his left pocket and give it to David Hale.

"A couple of times, Parker asked me to go out to the bait shop and get $120 in twenties, tens, usually small bills. I'd bring it in to the house, and Parker and David Hale would be sitting there, and I'd see Parker give it to David Hale. Sometimes it was only $40, $60, or $80 at a time, but other times it was $120 or $240 or $500. If Hale needed to pay a $200 bill, Parker would give him the money, plus an extra $100 or $120 for his pocket."[2] Hale denies taking any money, of course, and Dozhier denies giving it.
But keep reading, and then you decide.

Liar, Liar

Although Ken Starr has publicly deemed David Hale "truthful" and has even lobbied a judge on his behalf for a reduced sentence on his conviction for defrauding the federal government, Hale has several recurring outbreaks of dishonesty on his record. In fact, Hale has admittedly lied under oath to the FBI, the Small Business Administration, *and* a federal judge. Moreover, Hale has already served twenty months in the pokey.

Not exactly the poster boy for honesty, is he? Nevertheless, he has been the linchpin of the Whitewater investigation since its beginning, despite the fact that Hale made no mention of the President until several years after he was first questioned about the loan.[3]

You can imagine how easy Bill Clinton is to forget.

As Colin Capp, a juror in the McDougal Whitewater trial, put it, Hale is "an unmitigated liar [who] perjured himself. David Hale invoked the President's name for one reason: to save his butt. We all thought that way."[4]

I couldn't have said it better myself.

* * *

Now, let's stop and think about this for a moment. Despite the fact that he's a near pathological liar, David Hale's crazy comments have been the heart and soul of the endless Whitewater investigation. Now it appears that he may have been paid by the anti-Clinton right-wingers from the start!

Oh, but it gets worse.

According to *Salon*, two anonymous sources at *The American Spectator* also confirm that funds from the Arkansas Project went to Hale (although Boynton and *The American Spectator*'s publisher deny it). Moreover, when Ronald Burr, a founder and publisher of the *Spectator*, became concerned about the use of Arkansas Project money and attempted an outside audit, he was forced to submit his resignation. This audacious move prompted the departure of several *Spectator* writers in protest.

Burr was sworn to secrecy as part of his severance package, which was reportedly put together by *Spectator* board member and longtime Starr confidant Theodore Olson. (This is the same Ted

Olson who is now co-heading the magazine's "internal investigation" into the dark dealings of the Arkansas Project. Hmmm . . . something tells me he's not going to come up with anything.)

For his part, Parker Dozhier emphatically denies making any payments to Hale. When *Salon* reporters questioned Dozhier about the eyewitness account of Joshua Rand, however, the bait shop owner declared that the young man "was destined to be a chalk outline somewhere."

Are those the words of an innocent man?

Well, that threat sure didn't sit right with the Justice Department. Perturbed by these allegations of witness tampering, Deputy Attorney General Eric Holder has demanded that the independent counsel get to the bottom of this right-wing conspiracy tainting his investigation. And that's terrible news for the relentless Inspector Starr.

For one thing, the independent counsel must now investigate whether Richard Scaife, the financial benefactor behind his interrupted Malibu retirement plan at Pepperdine University, corrupted David Hale, Starr's prime Whitewater witness. Moreover, Starr must scrutinize the agenda of a magazine headed by Ted Olson, a man he admits is one of his best friends. And—here's the real kicker—since Mann and Rand claim that Hale was always accompanied by FBI agents, Starr must try to salvage the appearance of his own independence while interrogating his own staff!

The nature of these conflicts was not lost on the Justice Department. Although the independent counsel statute pretty much gave the department no choice but to hand this embarrassing investiga-

tion to Starr, the deputy attorney general nevertheless offered him an escape clause. In his letter to
Starr regarding the matter, Holder noted that
"there have been suggestions that your office
would have a conflict of interest, or at least the
appearance of a conflict," and that, if Starr felt
compromised in any way, he should hand the investigation back over to Justice.

For his own arcane reasons, Starr didn't bite. Rather,
he reaffirmed his independence and instead claimed that Janet
Reno's Justice Department, being part of the Clinton administration, had a much more dire conflict of interest than anything that
might stem from this "irrelevant" Hale situation.

Finally, in a compromise, Starr and the Justice Department
agreed on the appointment of Michael Shaheen, a former senior
Justice official, to investigate the independent counsel. (It's important to note that Shaheen will report to a panel of judges rather
than to Starr himself.)

As of this writing, the details of the alleged David Hale payoff
still remain murky. I can only hope that it takes fewer than four
years and less than $40 million before Ken Starr can explain all the
little quirks of the bait shop episode, including how his own
investigation became so enmeshed with claims of right-wing payoffs to key witnesses. Frankly, I don't think the American people
have the patience, pocketbook, or stomach for it.

Isn't it about time for the independent counsel to come clean?
The whole country needs to know what Ken Starr knew, and *when*
he knew it.

SWM Seeks WSJ

When Parker Dozhier wasn't cutting up local newspapers for *The American Spectator* and meeting with David Hale, he spent his free time playing cloak-and-dagger games with *The Wall Street Journal*. Dozhier, also known by the code name "Anne," would type up confidential grand jury information he obtained from Hale and leak it to reporters. Obviously a longtime fan of *Mission: Impossible*, "Anne" wore surgical gloves so as not to leave fingerprints on his typewriter keys. This budding master spy then sent the notes to prominent Whitewater reporters and encouraged them to communicate with him through the classifieds of the *Arkansas Democrat-Gazette*.

Apparently, the bait shop owner caught a couple of minnows. One reply, buried in the April 25, 1995, *Gazette* classifieds, read, "Anne—We got your message. We would love to hear from you. Bruce & Ellen." As it turns out, the New York telephone number left in the ad was that of Ellen Pollock, a reporter for *The Wall Street Journal*. Pollock covered Whitewater for the *Journal* along with a writer named Bruce Ingersoll.

Guess this might just explain *one* of the many leaks in the Whitewater sieve.

Why Bother with
Secret Payments?

No wonder Ken Starr never found the David Hale payola story very scintillating—Starr himself has been looking after the needs of his star witness, and not even bothering to use the cover of a bait shop. The independent counsel paid $68,000 of *taxpayer money* to Hale for his living expenses. In case you're curious, that $68,000 included $42,753.06 for lodging, $16,373.87 for food, $5,183.79 for auto maintenance, and $3,673.12 for "miscellaneous expenses," such as kitty litter.[5] He also paid for FBI agents to escort Hale to various social functions.

You know, you gotta wonder why the guy needed $5,000 to keep up his car when insurance records show that Parker Dozhier and the goons at the *Spectator* had already given his family use of an automobile. I guess he figured if the American taxpayers were footing the bill, he could finally afford that new car stereo. Rock on, David!

Follow the Money 2:

Arkansas Troopers and Right-Wing Payola

You know, these right-wing operatives are like cockroaches. If you find one, chances are there's a hundred more scuttling about doing their germy business. So it shouldn't come as much of a surprise that right-wing payola lies at the bottom of another of the so-called Clinton Scandals—Troopergate.

In December of 1993 the mighty *Los Angeles Times*, one of the most widely read and well-respected publications in the world, published a five-part story in which Arkansas state troopers made scurrilous allegations about the First Lady, and claimed that then Governor Clinton had used troopers to procure women for him.[1] In several front-page, above-the-fold stories, troopers Larry Patterson and Roger Perry wove a lurid tale of sex and power in the governor's mansion. (And, frankly, I don't think it speaks well of supposed journalistic impartiality that Doug Frantz, one of the writers of the *Times* articles, referred to Patterson and Perry on *Nightline* as "our troopers.")[2] The *Los Angeles Times* placed its considerable weight behind this story, and, before the ink had dried on the first edition, the networks were all over it: Ted Koppel, on *Nightline*, weighed in immediately.

Troopergate was on the lips of everyone at Georgetown cocktail parties, Washington power-dining establishments, and everywhere else that "important people" meet and discuss things in the District. And it did make a wonderfully compelling, if completely false, story: Courageous state troopers step forward to expose a sex-crazed governor and his overambitious wife, who used government employees—dedicated law enforcement officers—in pursuit of their sordid, twisted goals. All in all, it was a great day for the President's enemies and the media . . . except for the fact that one minor detail was, well, overlooked.

You see, these troopers had been bought and paid for with right-wing money.

In short, the *Los Angeles Times*, *Nightline*, and the rest of their kind were completely duped by the cockamamie crackpots of the right. Even more damning, once these pillars of journalism finally looked hard at the story and finally discovered the truth, they failed to take appropriate steps to notify their readers and viewers of how trumped up these stories had been.

But I'm happy to do their job for them (somebody's got to).

Here are the true facts surrounding the so-called Troopergate allegations:

FACT   *The troopers were paid off by a major Gingrich contributor.*

Peter W. Smith, a Chicago-based investment banker and a six-figure contributor to Newt Gingrich's GOPAC (GOP Political Action Committee), paid Patterson, Perry, and their lawyer $21,000 to spin the tale of Troopergate. This money was part of a full $80,000 spent by Mr. Smith to dredge up dirt on the Clintons, including the absolutely outrageous tale about the President fathering an illegitimate child by an Arkansas prostitute.

FACT   *The journalist who broke the story was also paid by Smith.*

American Spectator journalist David Brock, whose 1993 article on Troopergate first encouraged Paula Jones to make her case against the President, admits he was paid "research funds" by Peter Smith. Brock also notes that it was Smith who first introduced him to the disgruntled troopers. In an April 1998 *Esquire* column, Brock wonders if these "greedy" troopers with "slimy motives . . . took me for a ride."

Yes, indeed, Mr. Brock. The ride of your life.

FACT *The troopers also received money from one of the Reverend Jerry Falwell's organizations.*

Trooper Larry Patterson opened a joint bank account in 1995 with longtime Clinton-hater Larry Nichols. Money flowed into this account from the Jerry Falwell–backed Citizens for Honest Government, promoters of the absolutely hilarious, utterly crazy *Clinton Chronicles* video, a crackpot film that accuses the President of everything from cocaine smuggling to homicide. In turn, Patterson and Nichols confirm that they paid off at least six other people from this account. Now, maybe this is just a coincidence, but each of the six individuals who received that money also happened to have made allegations against the President.

FACT *Some Arkansas state troopers refute the tales told by their colleagues.*

Danny Ferguson and Ronnie Anderson, the two other Arkansas troopers who spoke to the *Los Angeles Times* and *The American*

Spectator, both disclaim the tales told by Patterson and Perry. Anderson said he had corroborated stories his colleagues told the press, even though he had no first-hand knowledge that they were true, and he has noted in a sworn affidavit that "the stories that were provided [by the troopers] were nothing more than old fish tales, with little, if any, basis in fact."[3]

Starr Wars:

The Independent Counsel's Abuses of Power

"Power tends to corrupt," Lord Acton said years ago, "and absolute power corrupts absolutely." Well, that old saw sure holds true for the esteemed independent counsel. Over the course of his four-year mission to destroy the President, Ken Starr has abused his power to such a degree and in so many different ways that it's a wonder he hasn't faced assault-and-battery charges.

Starr has never met a subpoena he didn't want to get his hands all over. He has badgered, intimidated, and harassed his witnesses and their families without remorse. He has trampled on and tried to eradicate every single legal privilege held by American citizens. And he has utilized every means and every sleazy technique in his repertoire to delve into the sex lives of his prey.

I am absolutely sickened by Inspector Starr's unconscionable and unprecedented abuse of power. As you might've guessed, I don't intend on keeping it a secret. And so, with another nod to Jack Webb, here's what the Carville Rapid Response Team has uncovered about the independent counsel's scandalous behavior and prosecutorial excesses. I'll also point out that, unlike the independent counsel's investigators, the Rapid Response Team didn't tread on a single civil right or intimidate any witnesses to expose these truths.

FACT *Ken Starr threatened Whitewater witness Sarah Hawkins with indictment, without evidence that she'd done anything wrong, in order to get her cooperation.*

The independent counsel's treatment of Arkansas native Sarah Hawkins is one of the worst examples around of the Starr approach to prosecution. After initially cooperating with Starr's investigators, Hawkins, a local Little Rock consultant, was told that if she didn't plead guilty to a felony, she would be indicted for bank fraud. When Hawkins refused Starr's ultimatum and professed her innocence, the independent counsel's investigators continued to threaten her with indictment and prosecution.

It was only after several months of torment, after Hawkins's reprehensible, criminal treatment by Starr's pack of prosecutorial dogs had caused her consulting business to evaporate, that investigators finally admitted they didn't have a drop of evidence to warrant her indictment. Not one molecule.

Even Sam Dash, the Watergate alumnus and Starr's hand-chosen ethics adviser, called the counsel's treatment of Sarah Hawkins "vicious." Nevertheless, that didn't stop Starr from trying a similar harassment routine on Webster Hubbell, Susan McDougal, Monica Lewinsky, and any other citizens unfortunate enough to interfere with his mission to bring down the President.[1]

FACT *Steve Smith says that Ken Starr's staff pressured him to testify about things that were untrue.*

Indeed, Sarah Hawkins was not the only one to receive the strong-arm from Starr's pit bulls. University of Arkansas professor Steve Smith, a longtime Clinton adviser who pled guilty to a misdemeanor related to the Whitewater deal, tells a similar grim tale about the counsel.

According to Smith, Starr's team encouraged him to lie to a grand jury about the Clintons' involvement in Whitewater. The script "contained things I had told them time and time again were not true," remembers the outraged Smith. "They kept trying to get me to say things that weren't true. They told me to sign a document they had written that was simply not true!" (Starr's deputy denies ever preparing such a script.)

Steve Smith was also the victim of another of Inspector Starr's favorite parlor tricks. Usually, if the independent counsel can't coerce his witnesses to lie by pressuring them individually, he generally follows that attempted coercion with threats to interrogate his victims' relatives instead. In Smith's case, Starr's team promised to browbeat his mother if Smith didn't play ball. "They said they were going to subpoena my mother, who was seventy years old and knew nothing," recalls the professor.[2]

FACT *Ken Starr subpoenaed a sixteen-year-old boy at his school in an attempt to intimidate him.*

Naturally, a prosecutor as heartless as Ken Starr doesn't stop at mothers alone. An IRS agent on Starr's squad was directed to serve Rob Hill Jr., a sixteen-year-old boy and the son of one of Starr's other targets, with a subpoena *at his school.* (Apparently for Starr, getting an education isn't nearly as important as getting the President.) The boy's lawyer said, justly and with admirable understatement, that Starr's actions were "meant to intimidate."[3]

FACT *Ken Starr kept Susan McDougal in jail for eighteen months because she would not testify to an affair he claimed she had with the President.*

One of the most heroic and long-suffering characters in the independent counsel's never-ending drama has been Susan McDougal. Despite all the underhanded tactics employed by Ken Starr to coerce McDougal into misrepresenting the involvement of the Clintons, she has stood her ground. She was locked up for almost two years because she refuses to alter facts for the Inspector's investigation. She's been separated from her family. She's been kept in the dingiest prisons possible and paraded around on camera in hand-cuffs *and a belly chain,* as if she were Hannibal Lecter.

And for what purpose has the esteemed Inspector gone to such lengths to intimidate Susan McDougal? Apparently to convince her to lie about her relationship with the President. As she puts it, "Jim McDougal, my ex-husband at the time, came to me and even asked me to say that I'd had an affair with the President. He said that I could write my own ticket if I would say such a thing. . . . If I would say that I had had an affair with the President, that would be enough for me to get a deal from them."[4]

Now, why on earth would Ken Starr want Susan McDougal to claim she had an affair with the President? And what in God's name could that have to do with the Whitewater case anyway? I guess the lascivious-minded independent counsel just can't miss an opportunity to delve into somebody's sex life, even if that sex life has been invented by the flunkies in his office.

FACT *Ken Starr's investigators were scrounging for dirt on alleged Clinton affairs long before the Monica Lewinsky allegations.*

Even before this tawdry new phase of the independent counsel's persecution began this year, Ken Starr had spent quite a bit of time, on the public payroll, snouting through the President's private life.

Legendary Watergate reporter Bob Woodward reported in June of 1997 that, while Starr and his lackeys were theoretically investigating Whitewater for a third year, what they were in fact doing was questioning the President's Arkansas associates—and any Little Rock woman they could put their hands on—about the President's sex life. As one Arkansas trooper recalls, "In the past, I thought they were trying to get to the bottom of Whitewater. . . . This last time, I was left with the impression that they wanted to show he was a womanizer. . . . All they wanted to talk about was women."[5]

At the time, many members of the press were outraged by Starr's sexual hang-up. The *Boston Globe* remarked that the counsel's conduct "offends common sense . . . [and] has the look of a dirty trick," while the *Los Angeles Times* declared that Starr's actions "threaten to set an ugly and undesirable precedent for future investigations." Even *Newsweek* reporter Michael Isikoff, Lucianne Goldberg buddy and breaker of the Lewinsky story, thought that Starr's team had "overstepped their bounds" and that their sex-police bit was "probably the most serious mistake that was made by his office."[6]

But, predictably, when the Lewinsky scandal broke, many of the same press organizations that had criticized Starr in 1997 were sniffing at his door for salacious gossip, scuttlebutt, and hearsay in 1998.

Ain't that always the way.

Oscar Wilde once said, "A man who moralizes is usually a hypocrite." Now I know he wasn't thinking about Ken Starr, but he certainly could have been. We all know that while the meter has been running on this high-priced investigation, Ken Starr's been jetting around the country in the service of tobacco interests. But let's look at Ken Starr's moralizing in his now famous speech before the Mecklenburg Bar Foundation in North Carolina and compare it to the record of this high-minded lawyer:

QUOTE *"Now in contrast to this very noble and trustworthy soul, today's popular culture portrays lawyers as greedy and unethical people who will cheerfully hawk their services—and, indeed, their very morals—to the highest bidder."*

THE TRUTH Ken Starr was listed as lead counsel for the twelve tobacco companies seeking to decertify a massive class action against the tobacco industry in a June 1995 brief filed with the U.S. Court of Appeals in New Orleans.

QUOTE *"As the educator and lawyer Robert Maynard Hutchins once put it very well, 'There are some things a professional will not do for money.'"*

...And the Horse He Rode In On

THE TRUTH   Ken's hourly rate: $390.[7]

QUOTE   *"Lawyers have a duty not to use their skills to impede the search for truth."*

THE TRUTH   About Starr's tobacco work, Representative Henry Waxman said: "It is questionable for a special prosecutor to moonlight at all. But to front for the tobacco industry to stop the public from learning the truth is not helpful in insuring confidence in the highly political Whitewater case."[8]

Or perhaps this is the worst case: After so much money has been spent on Starr's prize witness, David Hale, you'd think Starr would have the courtesy to be there in the courthouse while Hale testified against the President. But Starr wasn't anywhere near. He was in New Orleans defending his client Brown & Williamson. Frank Rich had this to say: "Mr. Starr hocked his services to the highest bidder whose main goal is to impede, not further, the revelation of truth . . . that bidder was Brown & Williamson. . . . Mr. Starr was the lawyer who invoked attorney-client privilege, however irrelevantly, before an appellate court in 1995 to further his client's efforts to intimidate and frustrate Henry Waxman and Ron Wyden, who'd used a cache of Brown & Williamson internal documents in their House investigation of the cigarette industry. . . . The red-hot evidence Mr. Starr was trying to shield with attorney-client privilege and other legal red-herrings was of a possibly criminal conspiracy to destroy the health of millions of Americans. The Brown & Williamson documents suggested that the company had known that nicotine was addictive since 1963 and had suppressed research linking smoking to cancer and heart disease."[9]

I guess now we know where the purveyors of "today's popular culture" turn for their inspiration.

FACT *Starr's investigators harassed White House Interior Department liaison Bob Hattoy about recruiting gay people to work in the Clinton administration.*

In an April 1997 interview with Bob Hattoy, a gay activist and former White House employee, the Starr squad apparently asked him time and time again if he'd helped gays and lesbians achieve prominent positions in the Clinton White House, as if gays and lesbians somehow don't deserve equal treatment, employment, and opportunity in America.[10]

What in the world could the relevance of such questions have been in the first place? The answer lies only in the twisted mind of the dogged Inspector.

FACT *Ken Starr threatened and pressured Monica Lewinsky to cooperate for eight or nine straight hours without an attorney.*

I'm sure y'all have heard about this one by now. After wiring up her best friend (the conniving, self-serving Linda Tripp), setting up a Pentagon City sting operation, and closing in on her like she was a drug kingpin, Starr's team and their FBI goons held Monica Lewinsky at a hotel for nearly half a day, with no legal representation, and tried to scare her into their version of playing ball. Just the thought of all those grown men browbeating a young woman for hours on end in a hotel room (!?) gives me the creeps. If it had been one of my daughters Starr had held captive, let me tell you, there would've been hell to pay.

Of course, these kinds of Orwellian intimidation tactics have been Starr's modus operandi from Day One—whether it's dragging Susan McDougal around in handcuffs and a belly chain or compelling Monica Lewinsky to give voice, fingerprint, and writing samples to the FBI as if she were some mobster. As William Ginsburg, Lewinsky's former attorney, put it, "Repeatedly during discussions with [Starr] we have been squeezed. . . . The Office of the Independent Counsel [has an] orchestrated campaign to pressure Ms. Lewinsky into statements that are not true."[11]

FACT *Ken Starr subpoenaed White House aide Robert Weiner simply for calling some friends on Super Bowl Sunday.*

While Bob Weiner, a spokesperson for Clinton drug czar Barry McCaffrey, was watching one of the best Super Bowls ever this past January, he called a few Maryland Democrat friends of his to congratulate them on their demands for an investigation into Linda Tripp's illegal telephone recordings. Faster than you could say "The AFC is back," Ken Starr had subpoenaed Weiner for having the audacity to call his friends on Super Bowl Sunday.

Be warned, folks: If you let your fingers do the walking, Ken Starr will let his subpoenas do the talking.

FACT *Ken Starr subpoenaed Marcia Lewis, Monica Lewinsky's mother, and harassed her for two days.*

Although Department of Justice guidelines suggest that close relatives should not be forced to testify against family members, Ken Starr didn't hesitate to drag Marcia Lewis into court for hours on end in yet another attempt to intimidate Lewinsky. In fact, Lewis was supposed to go in for a third day of the Starr treatment, but was made too ill by the first forty-eight hours of harassment to continue. Attorney William Ginsburg put this nasty episode in its proper perspective: "It's not nice. It's ugly. And all Americans should take note of how far they are going."[12]

FACT *Ken Starr's investigators, bearing guns and badges, interrogated Lewinsky's younger brother at his fraternity house.*

Heck, they act like a lynch mob, so why not look the part? Starr's team tried to threaten Monica's brother Michael into submission by dropping in on him at his Carnegie Mellon University fraternity house and showing off their weapons.[13]

FACT *Ken Starr went after Monica Lewinsky before receiving the proper authorization from the Justice Department.*

You do the math. Starr wired up Linda Tripp to entrap Monica Lewinsky on Tuesday, January 13, but didn't ask for permission to investigate Monica Lewinsky until Friday, January 16. (All right, I'll do the math: That's three days after the fact.) The independent counsel conducted his going-after-the-mob-style sting operation on a young woman before he had any God-given right, or at least permission from the Justice Department, to do so!

I just can't figure this guy. What kind of supposedly "impartial" investigator would go to such absurd lengths to get the President?[14]

FACT *Ken Starr subpoenaed the bookstore where Monica Lewinsky shopped.*

In another blatant attack on the Constitution by the independent counsel, Starr subpoenaed two Washington bookstores—Barnes & Noble and Kramerbooks—for Monica Lewinsky's book purchase receipts, presumably to ascertain her reading habits. This astonishing move rightfully stirred up a hornet's nest of criticism from publishers, librarians, and booksellers alike from around the country.

Starr's tactic "smacked of some of the worst abuses under a totalitarian regime," said the national director of Americans for Democratic Action. "This is a scenario that belongs in Baghdad or Tehran," noted Patricia Schroeder, former congresswoman and current head of the Association of American Publishers. "I don't think the American people could find anything more alien to our way of life or more repugnant to the Bill of Rights than government intrusion into what we think or what we read."[15]

They're absolutely right. But apparently the esteemed Inspector doesn't mind if the end result of his partisan persecution is a chilling effect on intellectual freedom in America. If his prying into bookstore receipts bothers you as much as it did me, I strongly encourage you to buy multiple copies of both this and my previous book, *We're Right, They're Wrong,* and send your receipts to the Office of the Independent Counsel.

My Reading List

Hey, put that subpoena away, Mr. Starr. I'd be glad to tell you what books I've been reading lately (although, if you put me on the stand, I'm gonna have to admit I only read the Cliffs Notes).

- *Les Misérables* by Victor Hugo: The obsessive Inspector Javert will stop at nothing in his single-minded quest to bring down an innocent man.
- *The Crucible* by Arthur Miller: Salem, Massachusetts, is turned upside down and innocent people are put to death when the sanctimonious Judge Hathorne forsakes law for zealotry.
- *Moby-Dick* by Herman Melville: Captain Ahab slowly degenerates and is ultimately consumed by his obsessive mission to hunt down a great and noble creature.

FACT *Ken Starr subpoenaed a decorating store where Webster Hubbell shopped.*

You think subpoenaing bookstores is hard to defend? Try this one on for size. Susan Pfeifer, the owner of Design Center, a Little Rock home-decorating store, was forced to spend more than a week of her time responding to a Starr subpoena requesting the records of all purchases by Webster Hubbell. "They wanted to know his buying habits, and so we were taking boxes of credit-card receipts home at night," remarked Pfeifer. "We came up with about $1,000 [in sales receipts] over five years. I was really outraged."[16]

It's a wonder Ken Starr didn't try to indict Hubbell for his taste in wallpaper. But who knows? Maybe after Webb's dog testifies, that's next.

FACT *Ken Starr subpoenaed a Florida television station for its videotapes of a trip to that state by the President.*

Also belonging to the grasping-at-straws department is the subpoena Ken Starr's office laid on a Florida television station for "videotape or tapes depicting President William Jefferson Clinton with Ms. Monica Lewinsky on a trip President Clinton made to Florida during which he visited with golfer Greg Norman." (That was also the trip during which the President wrenched his knee.) Not only did the television station *not* find any tape containing Lewinsky, it turns out she was never listed on White House travel records for the trip at all! Lewinsky had about as much chance of showing up on those tapes as Barney Fife.

"It was really reckless and irresponsible," noted the station's lawyer. "The most basic and obvious [investigation] would find there is no reason for this subpoena and that she did not come on this trip."[17]

Vox Populi

Last time I checked, the independent counsel was supposed to serve as a representative of the people. Well, Mr. Starr, the people have spoken. According to columnist Al Hunt, citing a June 1998 NBC/*Wall Street Journal* poll, "Nearly three-quarters of the respondents have little confidence that the report the independent counsel is expected to send to Congress will be fair and impartial." In fact, he continues, "even a majority of Republicans feel that way."[18]

If you're not a peacock-network fan, try this observation from a July 1998 Fox News poll on for size. According to Fox, when respondents were asked which of these events would likely occur first, 27 percent chose the end of Ken Starr's investigation; 58 percent chose the end of the millennium.

Just Following Orders:

Ken Starr's Underlings

Since Starr is the leader of this nasty little lynch mob, he naturally should take the lion's share of the blame for his investigation's abusive prosecutorial style. Nevertheless, a look at some of the independent counsel's minions will illustrate how Starr's abuses of power have reached such ridiculous, gutter levels. It seems that with Starr's underlings, the rotten apples don't thud too far from the tree.

Jackie Bennett

No surprise here: Starr's chief goon is as bullying and partisan as his master. Max Brantley, editor of the *Arkansas Times,* had this to say about Bennett, the independent counsel's head deputy: He "screams and berates witnesses. He's a schoolyard bully. Just about any defense attorney in Little Rock came away from Bennett feeling they'd been abused or worse. Bennett and his people sent FBI agents to a high school to get a yearbook picture of somebody. They brought in Jim Guy Tucker's stepson to rake him over the coals about what he'd heard at the dinner table."

Sounds like a real stand-up guy, doesn't he? Even his buddies, who claim that "Jackie sees his job as making people squirm," call him "unusually aggressive."[1]

In fact, even before he teamed up with Ken Starr some pretty heady individuals in the legal world noted Bennett's seriously screwed-up priorities. Gerald Goldstein, a former president of the National Association of Criminal Defense Lawyers, called Bennett "a bully" who "trampled on an individual's rights" in a 1992 election fraud case. (Bennett fell back on Starr's favorite routine: harassing innocent people in the hope of intimidating them.) In that same case, U.S. District Judge Lucius Bunton chastised Bennett for his "rinky-dinky case." As the judge put it to Bennett, the Justice Department could find "a hell of a lot better things to do with your time than sending you down here on a witch hunt."[2]

Ken Starr took that hint, but, as usual, he took it the wrong way: He assigned Bennett to an even bigger witch hunt.

Hickman Ewing

You know, of all of the independent counsel's cronies, I think I like Hickman Ewing the best. Because sometimes (not too often), he lets just a little bit of honesty slip out.

Like Ken Starr and Jackie Bennett, Ewing is as partisan as they come. But at least he has the courage to admit it. He told *The New*

Yorker in 1996 that, when investigating the President and First Lady, he operates from a presumption of guilt: "After you've been doing this for 10, 15, 20 years, it doesn't take too long to determine whether somebody has committed a crime."[3] Moreover, he has admitted to fellow lawyers that "the problem" with Whitewater is that "Ken wants to indict everyone for everything."[4] Ewing was also the inside man who explained the official Office of the Independent Counsel (OIC) leaking process to reporter Dan Moldea.

How can you not love this guy?

And here's the real kicker. It turns out that Hickman Ewing may be a connection between Starr's team and Richard Scaife's Arkansas Project. Although both Starr and Ewing have emphatically declared that "none of our people had any knowledge of payments" to Whitewater witness David Hale, Hickman reportedly met several times off the record with Rex Armistead, a Scaife-funded private investigator whom Ewing had known for many years. Though it's not clear what the two talked about or whether Ewing knew about Armistead's Scaife-funded dirty work making hay out of the old story about Governor Clinton helping cocaine runners in rural Arkansas, it is entirely conceivable that Armistead filled the OIC in on the Arkansas Project's alleged payoffs to Hale. As one federal investigator put it, "This [the meeting between Ewing and Armistead] was either the worst case of judgment, or something worse. But whatever it was, it needs to be looked at."[5]

Bruce Udolf

Yep, Udolf is another of Starr's deputies with a solid history of harsh prosecutorial behavior. In fact, Udolf was hit with a $50,000 civil judgment ($2,500 in compensatory damages and $47,500 in punitive damages) for violating a man's civil rights. Apparently, in 1985 Udolf locked up a carpenter named Richard Reeves for four days on a false gun charge without a bail hearing or access to a lawyer. True to form, Udolf was trying to build a case against Reeves's employer and decided he'd go about it by squeezing the little people who got in his way. Team Starr evidently heard about this $50,000 blot on Udolf's record and figured he was a must-have prosecutor for their out-of-control goon squad.

Michael Emmick

Michael "Runnin' Amok" Emmick, a former U.S. attorney in Los Angeles, was the fellow who cobbled together the Linda Tripp trap on Monica Lewinsky, and subsequently tried to pressure Lewinsky to testify against the President before her lawyer was present. Like Udolf, Emmick has a past as a truly persecutorial prosecutor. In one case, when a Ms. Christina Townley refused to testify against her ex-husband, a Los Angeles Police Department officer, in a corruption case in 1995, Emmick did everything in his power to intimidate and pressure her, including dredging up tapes in which she admitted she spoke of having an affair (which she denied under oath).

Eventually, as he would do later with the badly abused Webb Hubbell, Emmick tried to prosecute Townley on a tax-evasion charge for not playing ball. That time around, however, a federal judge threw out the case, saying that Emmick's prosecution style of "threats, deceit, and harassment techniques" was "callous, coercive, and vindictive."[6]

What's the Frequency, Kenneth?:

Ken Starr's Chronic Media Leaks

If Ken Starr had to pick his absolute *favorite* misuse of power as an independent counsel, I'd bet my life it'd be press leaks. I mean, the last man who leaked as much as Starr was poor old Sonny Corleone in the first *Godfather* movie.

And at least with respect to grand jury testimony, leaking information is illegal. Spelled out in concrete language in Rule 6E of the Federal Rules of Criminal Procedure is this little gem: "A grand juror, an interpreter, a stenographer, an operator of a recording device, a typist who transcribes recorded testimony, *an attorney for government,* or any person to whom disclosure is made under paragraph (3)(A)(ii) of this subdivision *shall not disclose matters occurring before the grand jury. . . .* A knowing violation of Rule 6 *may be punished as a contempt of court* [my italics]."

In fact, *Legal Times* magazine raised the bar on the interpretation of that statute even further, writing that "Any disclosure of grand jury material, known as a 6E violation, is considered a *federal crime*. Leaking this confidential information is also a violation of Justice Department guidelines, American Bar Association model rules, and D.C. Bar ethics rules."[1]

Federal crime or not, the independent counsel seems to be spewing self-serving information like the *Exxon Valdez* oil tanker. As Harvard professor Alan Dershowitz succinctly put it, "Material is just not safe once it gets in the presence of this independent counsel's office."[2]

But don't hate Ken Starr for it—he just can't resist. Why miss a chance to smear your enemies *and* get your name in the papers at the same time? Betcha can't leak just once, Inspector!

A Starr Turn from the Pages of Richard Nixon

Ken Starr has said that he "really identified with Nixon" in the 1960 Kennedy-Nixon television debates. Evidently so. The following excerpts from Nixon's White House tapes, as transcribed by Stanley I. Kutler in his book *Abuse of Power,* shed light on the origins of our Starr player's modus operandi.[3]

Nixon to Bob Haldeman, Charles Colson, John Ehrlichman, July 1, 1971
"I don't want that fellow Ellsberg to be brought up until after the election. I mean, just let—convict the son of a bitch *in the*

press. That's the way it's done. . . . Nobody ever reads any of this in my biographies. Go back and read the chapter on the Hiss case in *Six Crises* and you'll see how it was done. It wasn't done waiting for the Goddamn courts or the attorney general or the FBI."

Nixon to Haldeman and Henry Kissinger, July 1, 1971
"Let me show you what happened [in the Hiss case]. . . . I played it in the press like a mask. I leaked out the papers. I leaked everything. I mean, everything that I could. I leaked out the testimony. I had Hiss convicted before he ever got to the grand jury."

Nixon to Haldeman and Kissinger, July 1, 1971, on getting Daniel Ellsberg
"I mean, we will leak—we're going to leak out bits and pieces. . . . The conspiracy. All at once we find with regard to the conspiracy there's going to be leaked to columnists and we'll kill these sons of bitches. This [NSC official] Cooke, I want to get him killed. Let him get in the papers and deny it."

Ken Starr's Likely Leaks

And so with Master Leaker Richard Nixon's words echoing in our ears (no wonder he needed all those Plumbers), let's take a look at the wet work in the press, along with some ideas about the motivations for the leaks.

LEAK #1
Starr investigating suspension of three RTC officials (12/8/94)

"Three sources familiar with the investigation" all speaking "on the condition that they may not be identified by name" told the Associated Press that Starr was scrutinizing several investigators at the Resolution Trust Corporation (RTC) about their internal Whitewater probe.[4]

Why make this leak?

In case you forgot, this is the same RTC that happened to be suing Starr's law firm at the same time the independent counsel was raking it over the coals. Good idea to put more heat and pressure on these folks by leaking their names to the media, huh?

LEAK #2
First Lady's fingerprints on Rose Law Firm billing records (5/6/96)

"Sources close to the inquiry" told the amazingly well-connected Michael Isikoff of *Newsweek* magazine that "FBI experts" identified the First Lady's fingerprints on the billing records of the Rose Law Firm.[5] The firm, Mrs. Clinton's law firm, has been accused of illegal billing practices.

Why?

With this leak, Starr's team was trying to publicly brand the First Lady as a liar attempting to conceal evidence of wrongdoing.

Basically, they wanted to make the case that the First Lady was trying to hide information from investigators.

Naturally, what was left out of the story is the fact that fingerprints can last up to twenty years, and that it's impossible to tell exactly when the First Lady touched these documents. In fact, Mrs. Clinton has said several times that she may have used these papers during the 1992 campaign in order to respond to press inquiries. But that small factual glitch in the story didn't stop Starr's posse from launching its smear salvo.

LEAK #3   *"Fifty-fifty" chance the First Lady will be indicted (4/22/96)*

In a 1996 *New Yorker* article, journalist Jane Mayer quoted a *"top official with the [Starr] investigation"* as saying there was a "fifty-fifty" chance that the First Lady would be indicted by the independent counsel for crimes relating to Whitewater.

Why?

Same dirty tricks as above. An easy chance to defame Mrs. Clinton.

Since there's still no evidence of wrongdoing by the First Lady (even two years after this unconscionable leak), this comment was wildly off the mark. Of course, that didn't mean that that contemptible allegation wasn't the talk of the town for the next year. Press people, including such esteemed pundits as William Safire, Fred Barnes, and Stuart Taylor, actually repeated this crazy claim as if it were holy writ.[6]

...And the Horse He Rode In On

Indeed, CBS News cited "*two lawyers familiar with the investigation*" as making the same remark nine months later.[7] Apparently, Starr was working to keep the fires stoked (without getting his hands dirty, of course). Howard Kurtz, a *Washington Post* reporter who remains one of the handful of D.C. journalists unsullied by the media's recent descent into spectacle and hearsay, characterized this well-executed piece of character assassination best. "Now I know this is terribly old-fashioned," he remarked, "but I don't think that journalists ought to quote unnamed prosecutors as saying they have enough to charge somebody if those prosecutors don't want to go on the record or bring a charge. *This is the classic case of trying someone in the press* [my italics]."[8]

We could sure use more old-fashioned journalists around here these days.

LEAK #4   President's purported relationship with Dan Lasater probed (11/6/95)

Insight magazine, an offshoot of the right-wing *Washington Times*, reported that "*sources close to the Starr investigation*" were "intrigued" by the President's ties to Dan Lasater, an Arkansas man who was the target of federal and state drug probes. Apparently, then Governor Clinton aggressively lobbied the Arkansas legislature in 1986 to approve a $30 million bond issue for a new police radio system being marketed by Lasater. According to the unnamed sources, Starr's team was questioning state troopers about the "friendship" between the governor and Lasater.[9]

Why?

A blood-simple smear, and the chance to indirectly associate the President with the word "drugs."

The story neglected to mention some important earlier reporting on the subject by CNN. According to the news network, Lasater had not spoken to the President since 1986, and in fact had only met Mr. Clinton a handful of times. Moreover, the Arkansas lawmakers lobbied by Clinton all state that his support was solely for the communications project, not for Lasater himself.[10]

LEAK #5   *President Clinton pressured Hale to make loans (10/19/94)*

In October 1994, the *Washington Times* reported that, according to *"law enforcement"* sources, Arkansas state trooper L. D. Brown told investigators that he overheard the President ask David Hale to arrange the bad $300,000 loan at the center of Whitewater.[11]

Why?

Probably to gather some momentum for Starr's sputtering Whitewater investigation. Perhaps the independent counsel wanted to set up the pretext for one of his many "critical phases."

Nevertheless, as I noted earlier, David Hale lies like a cheap rug on a warped floor, and, to this day, no one has corroborated his story.

...And the Horse He Rode In On

LEAK #6 — *Investigation of Vincent Foster's suicide (11/20/95)*

"A source close to the investigation" told the *Washington Times* in 1995 that Ken Starr "may seek to exhume the body of Vince Foster" to conclusively discern the cause of his death. This would have marked "an about-face by Starr, who was about to conclude Foster had killed himself."[12]

Why?

Because anti-Clinton crazies and the black-helicopter conspiracy crowd have always had a soft spot for this cruel falsehood. Why not throw the rabid dogs a bone?

Eventually, after the President had won a second term and public trust in Ken Starr had begun to falter (thanks in part to his abrupt decisions to resign from, then return to, his post), the independent counsel finally "concluded," as had the investigations of previous independent counsel Robert Fiske, Pennsylvania Republican Representative Bill Clinger, and *60 Minutes* before him, that Vince Foster had indeed committed suicide.

LEAK #7 — *Bruce Lindsey to be indicted (11/13/95)*

In 1995, *Insight* magazine (isn't it strange how, of all the newspapers and magazines in the world, it's usually this right-wing rag that gets all the dirty scoops about Starr's work?) reported that "Bruce Lindsey, a Clinton aide and intimate friend of the First

Family, still is being scrutinized. There is a fifty-fifty chance that he will be prosecuted for banking and tax violations."[13]

Why?

A chance to smear another Clinton aide, and, thus, indirectly smear the President.

Hmmm... there're those fifty-fifty odds again. Since they never had any evidence in the first place, it seems possible that Starr's team uses another fifty-fifty proposition—flipping a coin—to choose whom to indict. At any rate, more than two years have passed since this story "broke," and Bruce Lindsey has yet to be indicted for one damn thing.

LEAK #8   *Whitewater documents stored in Clinton-Gore campaign headquarters (1/15/96)*

As reported by the *Washington Times* in 1996, *"sources close to the Starr inquiry"* claimed that documents related to Whitewater were moved out of the Rose Law Firm to the Clinton-Gore campaign headquarters in downtown Little Rock.[14]

Why?

To show that those evil, scheming Democrats are always up to no good.

Now, if you've seen *The War Room*, the documentary by Chris Hegedus and D. A. Pennebaker about the 1992 Clinton campaign, you'll know that I have a soft spot for those Little Rock headquarters. Come on, Mr. Starr, I realize you probably can't help yourself anymore, but do you really have to drag the War Room into your pathetic Whitewater web? Man, talk about your sore losers.

LEAK #9   *Papers removed from Vincent Foster death scene (11/6/95)*

The reporters at the *Washington Times* must get sick of always having to beat around the bush. *"According to sources"* in 1995, "some of Starr's investigators are speculating that papers, possibly even a briefcase, were hustled away from the death scene [of Vincent Foster] or grabbed from Foster's vehicle before the Park Police arrived."[15] Richard Mellon Scaife's pet reporter, Christopher Ruddy of the *Pittsburgh Tribune-Review,* reported a similar story a few months later, with the help of *"two sources close to Starr's probe."*[16]

Why?

Like I said before, Starr's squad loved to get some mileage out of the Vince Foster conspiracy theories.

I dunno, but this sounds kinda paranoid to me. The only place I ever saw Vince Foster's briefcase was in the hands of Republican Senator Frank Murkowski, who began the GOP Senate hearings on the Foster suicide by tactlessly waving it around like a bloody flag. Naturally, the briefcase was on loan from the office of Ken Starr.

LEAK #10 *Webster Hubbell investigation (11/24/94)*

The *Los Angeles Times* claimed on November 24, 1994, that *"sources close to the case"* reported that Starr would indict Webster Hubbell over allegations of financial irregularities. On December 3, 1994, the day after Hubbell pled guilty to two such felonies, the *Washington Times* quoted *"a source close to the Whitewater probe"* as saying that "Webb Hubbell could be the John Dean of Whitewater." The article went on to say that *"sources close to the investigation"* had outlined the various ways in which Hubbell's plea bargain aided the Starr investigation.[17]

Why?

Forget about Hubbell being the John Dean of Whitewater—with this leak, Ken Starr wanted to come off as the *James Dean* of independent counsels. (Call it *Rebel Without a Conscience*.) Not content to let the guilty plea speak for itself, Starr's whippin' boys even "outlined" for reporters how best to put a pro-Starr spin on events. The Inspector evidently wanted to announce to the world the next of his many "critical phases" of his investigation.

LEAK #11 *Money diverted in Arkansas prison bond deal (4/3/96)*

"Sources close to the probe" told (guess who?) the *Washington Times* that "Whitewater investigators have focused on the sale of tax-exempt bonds to finance a $13.9 million Arkansas prison, trying

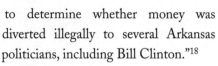

to determine whether money was
diverted illegally to several Arkansas
politicians, including Bill Clinton."[18]

Why?

Because they love to smear more
than two kids in a mud fight. This time
the implication is that the President may
have been stealing money from prisons.
Since this hokey allegation hasn't been mentioned again in the two years since this article
first ran, you have to assume Starr was once again shooting blanks.

What this wacky prison tale has to do with the Whitewater
land deal is beyond me.

LEAK #12   *Clinton campaigns gave money to black ministers (1/29/95)*

This time around *"sources familiar with [Starr's] probe"* told the
Washington Post (the *Washington Times* guy must have had the day
off) that the independent counsel was investigating possible improper payments to black ministers by Bill Clinton's Arkansas
gubernatorial campaigns.[19]

Why?

Like the prison story before, it's just another brainless, uncor-
roborated smear. This one's over three years stale, so once again I'm
assuming the inspector's teams didn't have the goods.

But here's a troubling thought: You ever notice how when

Republicans can't find anything, they always go after black folks? Well, guys, you can't fool a son of Louisiana with the oldest hate tactic in the book. I've seen it too many times before and I know exactly what you're up to.

* * *

Well, if you thought that was a lot of leaking by the good Inspector's office, let me tell you: The old boy outdid himself in the post-Lewinsky phase of his perpetual investigation. Once the media's round-the-clock "Clinton Scandal/Crisis in the White House/Investigating the President!!" campaign began, daily torrents of info and innuendo were spewed all over the place.

In those first few weeks of the frenzy, it didn't matter how ridiculous the claim or how privileged the information—Starr's team seemed to spoon as much bloody chum in the water as they could to keep the media sharks interested.

As a result of the press hysteria, the independent counsel no longer had to rely solely on his old pals at the *Washington Times* to spread the hateful innuendos. Driven stark raving mad at the thought of landing any kind of scoop, the most dutiful watchdogs of the press, including those pillars of journalism the *New York Times* and *Washington Post*, were now more crazed than ever to lap up the leaks.

Here's a humble sampler of them. And note the cagey language employed by most papers to cover up their sources.

LEAK #13 *Starr subpoenas Revlon's Ronald Perelman*
(1/27/98)

From the *New York Post:* Columnist Neal Travis reported that *"sources in Starr's office told me yesterday"* that the independent counsel was planning to subpoena Ronald Perelman, the Revlon CEO who chose Vernon Jordan for his company's board.[20] (To his credit, Travis is one of the few reporters bold enough to explicitly state the "contributions" of Starr's team.)

LEAK #14 *Bruce Lindsey reference on Tripp's tapes*
(1/29/98)

From the *New York Times: "A lawyer involved in the investigation* said that Lewinsky referred to [Bruce] Lindsey on one of the tapes [of her conversations with her co-worker Linda Tripp]."[21]

LEAK #15 *Starr's strategy is to "get" President Clinton*
(1/29/98)

From the *New York Daily News:* "Independent Counsel Kenneth Starr's strategy, *said a source close to his investigation*, is to have Lewinsky's grand-jury testimony contradict Clinton's sworn deposition in the Paula Jones sexual-harassment lawsuit."[22]

LEAK #16 *Starr seeking obstruction and conspiracy information (1/29/98)*

From the *Washington Times:* "*According to lawyers and others close to the probe,*" prosecutors were seeking information on Monica Lewinsky's role and that of others in an attempt to obstruct justice and to conspire to suborn perjury in her January 7 affidavit in the Jones case.[23]

LEAK #17 *Vernon Jordan job assistance (1/23/98)*

Starr's prosecutors evidently fed reporters details of Monica Lewinsky's story well before her testimony. According to the *New York Daily News*, "*Prosecutors* painted a different picture. 'Monica says . . . that she dealt directly with the President, who set the assistance in motion,' one *lawyer said, speaking on condition of anonymity.*"[24]

LEAK #18 *Starr to wire Lewinsky and tape the President (1/23/98)*

Although Ken Starr now denies it, "*Sources familiar with the probe* said Starr wanted the ex-intern to wear a secret recording device and discuss first with Jordan and then with Clinton why she should lie to Jones' lawyers," according to the *New York Daily News.*[25]

Associates in Ken Starr's office, hungry to keep the Inspector's media buddies in the leak loop, gave the *Washington Times*, in late January of this year, the inside track on information pertaining to Monica Lewinsky's bid for immunity. The *Times* declared that "*Sources close to independent counsel Kenneth W. Starr's Whitewater investigation* said the sticking point [in scheduling Lewinsky's Paula Jones deposition] involved specific terms of the immunity deal—her 'proffer.'"

The paper went on to parrot that "*Mr. Starr's staff* was described as believing it is a foregone conclusion she will eventually be granted immunity from prosecution for perjury, shielding Miss Lewinsky, 24, from felony charges that she falsely swore in an affidavit that she had no sexual relationship with the president."

Four days after that first story, the *Times* reported that "Monica Lewinsky offered last night to tell Whitewater independent counsel Kenneth W. Starr that she lied in a sworn affidavit denying a sexual relationship with President Clinton. . . . Miss Lewinsky agreed to cooperate in the counsel's probe in exchange for immunity in the case, *according to lawyers and others close to the Starr probe.* The written statement, or 'proffer,' was submitted after daylong negotiations. . . ."

"*Lawyers and others close to the Starr probe,*" the *Times* reported nine days later, said "Lewinsky submitted the written proposal [for a proffer agreement] to Whitewater prosecutors Monday night," February 2.[26]

LEAK #20 — *Defusing stories of prosecutorial abuse (1/24/98)*

The *Washington Post* reported that after Lewinsky's lawyer accused Starr and his investigators of trying to "squeeze" Lewinsky during an eight- or nine-hour interrogation session, *"sources close to Starr ... described a far different episode that dragged on mainly because Lewinsky insisted her mother be present. Although investigators did pressure her to cooperate, sources said, the onetime White House intern spent much of the time waiting for her mother to arrive."*[27]

LEAK #21 — *Mother puzzled that Lewinsky is the target of investigation (1/24/98)*

The *Washington Post* wrote that when Lewinsky's mother, Marcia Lewis, arrived from New York to counsel her daughter, Lewis did not understand why Lewinsky was in trouble. *"According to a source close to the prosecutors,"* Lewis was puzzled about why they were intent on making a criminal case at all, saying, "What's the big deal? So she lied and tried to convince someone else to lie."[28]

LEAK #22 — *The Kathleen Willey encounter (1/27/98)*

Details of President Clinton's alleged encounter with Kathleen Willey were leaked to the *Washington Times* by a *"source familiar*

with information sealed by the federal court in Richmond [Virginia]."
The *Times* claims that the info came from neither Willey's attorney nor Paula Jones's lawyers.[29]

Hmmm . . . that doesn't leave too many other possible sources to "credit," does it?

LEAK #23 *Starr sought Janet Reno's approval for political cover (1/23/98)*

The *Washington Post* reported that Starr did not need to get Reno's approval to expand his investigation into whether President Clinton was involved with Lewinsky. "But he wanted her approval for political reasons, to discourage Democrats from crying foul, said *a source close to the Starr probe.*"[30]

LEAK #24 *White House steward's access to Oval Office study (2/5/98)*

"Individuals familiar with Mr. Starr's inquiry," wrote *The Wall Street Journal,* "said his attorneys have questioned current and former White House aides during the past two weeks to determine whether Mr. Nelvis"—Bayani Nelvis, a White House steward—"would have access to the Oval Office and the adjacent study" (he did), "and whether he . . .witnessed a meeting between Mr. Clinton and Ms. Lewinsky" (he didn't).[31]

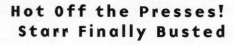

Hot Off the Presses!
Starr Finally Busted

How does Starr account for the multitude of leaks that seem to splash torrentially from his office? He can't. When questioned about leaking to the press, the independent counsel responded, "I do not have an explanation. I am very concerned."[32]

And, naturally, all of the righteous journalists suckling from the independent counsel's dribbling teat were loath to jump on Starr's flimsy answer and give up their sources.

Between Ken Starr talking out of the side of his mouth and the news outlets jumping on any leaks, whether sleazy or illegal, it was altogether possible that we would never know the truth behind all these unnamed sources.

Fortunately, though, one journalist finally had the temerity to step forward and explain how all this sensitive information had been coming out into the light of day. Dan Moldea, a respected crime reporter with more than seven exhaustively investigated books under his belt, heard one of Starr's emphatic denials and was so disgusted that he told his tale. According to Mr. Moldea:

"[Hickman] Ewing told me the process by which information is leaked out of the office of the independent counsel. He told me that yes, they do give information that is not on the public record on an off-the-record basis to selected reporters who are approved by Ken Starr in advance. He told me Ken Starr also approves specific leaks as long as the reporter's views are in sync with the office of the independent counsel's position. Our conversation took place on December 10, 1997, six weeks before the Lewinsky story broke."[33]

There it is, folks, in black and white. I guess that finally explains how the *Washington Times* ended up with so many scoops, doesn't it?

And if the word of Mr. Moldea wasn't proof enough, only a few weeks later an even more damning witness came forth to testify about the independent counsel's embarrassing leakage: *Ken Starr*. That's right, the good Inspector eventually became so blinded by his ego that he actually admitted to leaking like a rusty bucket.

In an interview with reporter Steven Brill for the premiere issue of *Brill's Content* magazine, the independent counsel announced that he and his chief partner-in-crime, Jackie Bennett, "have talked with reporters on background on some occasions," yet claimed there was "nothing improper" about discussing what witnesses tell FBI agents and other investigators before they testify in front of the grand jury.[34]

Uh, excuse me, Mr. Starr, lemme get this straight. Did you just freely admit that you—our esteemed, dispassionate, and "independent" counsel—have been leaking stories to the press? "That would be true," Starr backpedaled, "except in the case of a situation where what we are doing is countering misinformation that has been spread about our investigation in order to discredit our office and our dedicated career prosecutors. . . . We have a duty to promote confidence in the work of this office."[35]

Say what? What kind of cockamamie excuse is that? As this

book aims to illustrate, there's more than enough *information* in the air to completely discredit him and his right-wing operation. Starr doesn't need to fret about supposed *misinformation* when the *actual* information out there is so damning. For another thing, in at least one instance this guy was "countering misinformation" on the very day a particular story broke. No one could have created misinformation, because nobody even knew exactly what was going on!

You know, I find it just plain pathetic that this guy thinks he needs to promote confidence in a band of goons whose entire mission is to destroy the reputation of America's greatest President in decades. Seems to me they have an *over*confidence problem.

By the way, Mr. Starr, let me give you a friendly bit of advice: If you want to promote public assurance of the legitimacy of your investigation, it's probably best not to disclose to reporters that your modus operandi is pure sleaze and possibly illegal.

Ken Starr: Media Whore

Obviously, the independent counsel has no problem using his prosecutorial powers to get some good press. As it turns out, he doesn't mind abusing journalistic integrity or editorial powers either. While serving on the editorial board of the *American Bar Association (ABA) Journal*, Starr pushed the *Journal* to cover his Whitewater investigation. When the *Journal* finally did publish a piece questioning the right-wing origins of the independent counsel's appointment, Starr complained so much that reporter Henry Reske resigned his position with the *Journal* in disgust.[36]

Onward, Christian Soldier

Of all the leaks over these many years, this fantasy is above and beyond my favorite. Not long after Monica Lewinsky's arrival on the scene, the independent counsel's old buddies at the *Washington Times* published this sanctimonious laugher about a 1995 speech by Starr to the Christian Business Men's Committee. Entitled "Deeply Christian Starr Starts Day Jogging, Singing Hymns," the article ostensibly portrayed the private side of Ken Starr.

"My favorite [thing to do] is going on a morning jog—real early," recalled Starr. "I go right to the bank of Pimmit Run . . . I've got my favorite spot. And I sing a hymn. And I sing it aloud. Sometimes I'm huffing and puffing, but I sing it aloud. And then I offer a prayer."[37]

You see? Ken Starr isn't an out-of-control partisan persecutor. No, he's a devout, virtuous, and God-fearing warrior, come to bathe in the healing waters of the Potomac and smite all the sodomites and fornicators from Washington. My, what an illuminating piece of reporting. I guess that explains why, as White House aide Sidney Blumenthal noted in a speech at Harvard University, Starr has "jettisoned the language of the law, speaking now of 'defilers of the temple,' the apocalyptic rhetoric of the zealot, on a mission divined from higher authority."[38]

Now, when I made a similar comment about Starr's faith-healing jogs at a press breakfast, John Harris of the *Washington Post* asked if I was mocking Starr's religion. No, not at all. I was—and still am—mocking his self-piety. Being a Catholic from the old school, I learned more often from bishops than the Bible. But sometimes the Good Book just puts it all beautifully in perspective. And so I would refer our righteous Inspector to Matthew 6:5–6—"And when thou prayest, thou shalt not be as the hypocrites are: for they love to pray standing in the synagogues and in the corners of the streets, that they may be seen of men. . . . But thou, when thou prayest, enter into thy closet, and when thou hast shut thy door, pray to thy Father which is in secret; and thy Father which seeth in secret shall reward thee openly."

The Rabid Watchdog:

What Happened to Our Media?

Now, before I say anything about the declining state of our national press corps, I have to admit a few things. First off, to paraphrase Winston Churchill (who was talking about alcohol), in the end, I've taken more good from the press than the press has taken good from me. In all my years as a political consultant, working with reporters to get the message out has been my bread and butter. Plus, as you well know, I've logged my hours as a talking head during the past few years. Heck, I'm sure a lot of you are probably sick of hearing me hoot and holler every other Sunday morning by now. Moreover, I've got a lot of dear friends in the media business, and I would defy anyone who spoke ill of them.

That being said, something is seriously wrong at the old journalism factory these days. Former editor of *U.S. News & World Re-*

port James Fallows put it very well in his 1995 book *Breaking the News*. Like the army in the 1970s and the automobile industry in the 1980s, he noted, the national press of the 1990s refuses to recognize the clear evidence of its deterioration.

Or, put another way, the media has an important responsibility to act as our nation's dutiful watchdog. Unfortunately, this watchdog has gotten fleas, gone rabid, broken off of its chain, and is running around the country biting every outstretched hand.

Check out these facts. According to a study by the Committee of Concerned Journalists, as reported in the *International Herald Tribune*, more than 40 percent of news reports in the first five days of the media-manufactured Lewinsky crisis "consisted of analysis, opinion, and speculation, not factual reporting." Moreover, approximately 20 percent of the stories were "unverified by the news outlet reporting it and instead were taken from some other news outlet."[1] In other words, one out of every five journalists had no idea what they were talking about, and two out of every five reporters were making it up as they went along!

So with a nod to the *New York Times* (which used this same format to differentiate fact from fiction in one of the first Sunday editorials that recognized the pure godawfulness of the reporting on the Lewinsky crisis), here're some of the major aspects of the initial tale that the press, in its rush to make a fast buck through a faster scoop, got dead wrong[2]:

THE DECEIT

The President and Monica Lewinsky were seen in flagrante delicto by a Secret Service agent.

THE FACTS

This tall tale, first mentioned on television by reporter Jackie Judd of ABC News and in print by the *Dallas Morning News*, was a fixture on the scandal circuit in those first crazy days of Monica-mania. It was subsequently retracted by the *Morning News*. To this day, no Secret Service agent has ever stepped forward to tell that story. Journalist Steven Brill has speculated that this was an attempt by Ken Starr's office to pressure Lewinsky into playing ball.

THE DECEIT

A White House steward, Bayani Nelvis, testified that he had witnessed the President and Monica Lewinsky in a compromising position and that he had discovered semen-stained tissues in the trash.

THE FACTS

Ugh. What has happened to our society that we have to discuss such downright filth over morning coffee? At any rate, *The Wall Street Journal*, trying to make a splash on the Internet by posting this scoop on its Web site, is the media outlet that promoted this salacious number. However, after Mr. Nelvis's lawyer called the statement "absolutely false and irresponsible," the *Journal* was forced to retract it hours later, leaving only its editorial page to carry these derogatory and ridiculous comments about the President.

The President's Character

Well, you've probably figured out by now that I'm none too fond of Ken Starr. You want to know something else? I like Bill Clinton. I like his wife. I like his daughter. I loved his mother. I like his suck-down, spit-up view of life, whereby he stands by the little folks against the monied and powerful. I like his ideas. I like his employees. I like the way he listens to people. I like the way he helps people. I like his friends (to tell the truth, I don't care too much for a few folks in the Hollywood crowd, but that's his business). And I absolutely love the many things he's done to improve our country during his six years in office.

I mean, what's not to like? Here's a man who's been married to the same woman for decades (how many of the President's bitter-est critics can say the same?). He and his wife have successfully raised an exemplary young woman and been there for her every homework problem, piano practice, softball game, and ballet recital. He has been consistently kind to his friends and excellent to his employees. Here's a President who's had enough character to admit to the nation his imperfections and who has led us to an unparalleled era of prosperity with brilliance, intelligence, and compassion. Moreover, he has been the first President in a good long time who's had enough character to stand up for America's underdogs, the people in this country who most need standing up for.

Now, don't get me wrong. There are several of the President's enemies that I do respect and like. Many of Clinton's most vitriolic critics aren't venal, vicious, petty people—they're just wrong. Blinded by ideology and/or ambition, they refuse to admit both the many admirable traits in the President's character and the multitude of wonderful things he's done for America.

Yet, for years, these same poor, self-deluded fools have used every means at their disposal to accomplish what they twice couldn't do in an election—defeat Bill Clinton. And, in the end, after all of Inspector Starr's critical junctures, critical phases, and high-minded reflections on the truth, anybody with a grain of sense can see that this investigation is all about sex. Now, we've gotten to the point where these goons have spent $50 million of our money chasing four strands of DNA. This whole charade has become so offensive and stupid as to shake the conscience of any person. How so many bright, educated, and even well-meaning people could have such pathetic judgment as to portray these sex investigations as anything more than a half-baked attempt to take down the President is nothing short of a national disgrace.

The President's sex-obsessed enemies have succeeded in defining the word "character" down so that to them and the scandal-industry class it's become solely a code word for sex. Now, I'm not William Safire, but I think a better definition for character rests in the words of Civil War Lt. Col. Joshua Chamberlain, a four-term governor of Maine and Bowdoin College president who was wounded six separate times in battle. Chamberlain once defined character as "a firm and seasoned substance of soul," meaning "such qualities or acquirements as intelligence, thoughtfulness, conscientiousness, right mindedness, patience, fortitude, longsuffering and unconquerable resolve." In spite of all the despicably mean right-wing attacks of the past few years, the President has weathered the storm with patience, fortitude, and resolve. Throughout, the President has not only managed to do his job and bring our nation to new heights of prosperity, but has remained civil and even friendly to the vile, characterless monsters who have consistently abused his family.

Now, I'm kinda embarrassed to say this, but I've read a quote by Dante that puts this whole sex investigation in perspective (the way I figure it, why do I want to read about hell in this life when I'll be getting so much of it in the next?). In the *Inferno,* the Italian poet wrote, "Eternal Justice weighs the sins of the hot blooded and the cold hearted on different scales."

I'm sure y'all can tell that I'm a warm-blooded, passionate person, and I hope that God will judge me a compassionate person. And, in short, I love fellow warm-blooded, warm-hearted people. In my mind, an indiscretion here and an indiscretion there will never amount to a tenth of cruelty. A passionate indiscretion will never be judged in the same light as the sins of the cold-hearted and unforgiving. Do I wish everyone were pure and chaste all the time? Sure, but I would offer most people forgiveness and compassion regardless of what they did. In my heart of hearts, I have much more empathy, forgiveness, and love for those whose indiscretions arise from warm blood than for those whose indiscretions arise from a cold heart.

My good friend Tim Russert has portrayed this whole ugly episode as a "fight to the finish" between the President and the partisan persecutor, which will end with "one man standing." I agree. In fact, I would go so far as to say that this nasty moment in our history has become an epic battle between the warm-blooded and the cold-hearted. And, let me tell you, on every level I am proud to stand on the side of the warm-blooded.

If I let a friend of mine who has done such a great job in our highest office, a man who has twice been elected to that position, be run out of office and so consistently and viciously attacked by his enemies for some nickel-and-dime pissant sex charge, then there's something wrong with me. I would be nothing if I ran around with the vacuous, vapid talking-head class who'll say absolutely anything to get three minutes of cable airtime, including demeaning a man who's done so much for our nation. I've met Ken Starr and his peanut gallery of sycophantic talking heads, and I know Bill Clinton and his family, and I am proud beyond words to stand on the side of the President against the independent counsel.

In sum, character is not about perfection—it's about direction. For all his indiscretions, I believe Bill Clinton is a warm, compassionate human being who loves his family and his nation. If the

President's detractors had one tenth of his character, we would never have been subjected to this extended embarrassment of a sex investigation in the first place.

The GOP v. Larry Walsh

Ever since Ken Starr embarked on his latest rampage, the Republican Party has been denouncing folks like me for pointing out the fact that the independent counsel is a GOP hatchet man. For example, Speaker Gingrich has accused the President's defenders of "unpatriotically . . . undermining the Constitution of the United States" and being "demeaning" and "destructive."[1] My, how times change. Only six years ago, Speaker Newt and his cronies were rabidly attacking special counsel Lawrence Walsh, a man who is universally acknowledged to have executed his job with much more dignity and aplomb than Inspector Starr could ever muster:

Newt Gingrich: Newt was one of seventy-five House Republicans who signed a 1992 letter to then Attorney General William Barr asking him to conduct a "preliminary inquiry" into whether "Walsh . . . or any other employees of the Independent Counsel's office may have violated federal criminal law."[2]

Bob Dole: The former senator and GOP presidential candidate accused Walsh and his staff of blackmail and referred to the independent counsel's office as "highly paid assassins."[3]

Orrin Hatch: When it came to Larry Walsh, Senator Hatch could do a pretty convincing impression of me on Ken Starr. Hatch called Walsh's investigation a "tainted" case of "cruel and unusual punishment" that "started to look more like persecution than prosecution." Moreover, Senator Hatch derided Walsh's staff as "a bunch of hot-shot attorneys."[4] You know, it's just too bad old Orrin doesn't feel the same about the GOP's pet Starr—he's really got a way with words when it comes to independent counsels.

R.M. Scaife: Right-Wing Godfather

One of Richard Mellon Scaife's favorite anti-Clinton conspiracy theories over the years has been the "mysteries" surrounding the suicide of White House aide Vince Foster. Scaife has exercised his considerable financial leverage many times to promote the highly dubious and consistently discredited theory that Foster was murdered, including helping to finance one of his pet reporters, Christopher Ruddy, in his dogged coverage of the subject.

Why is Scaife so intrigued by Foster's death? A look into the right-wing godfather's past may reveal an unsettling answer. In the 1960s, Scaife publicly supported Robert Duggan, a candidate for district attorney with strong reformist credentials. However, Scaife had an abrupt falling out with Duggan in 1973 after Duggan was under investigation for corruption. Duggan then eloped with Scaife's sister, Cordelia.

A few months later, Duggan was found dead, apparently of a self-inflicted shotgun blast. The alleged suicide weapon was found devoid of fingerprints, several feet from Duggan's body, causing many to wonder whether it was really a suicide. If that isn't strange enough, to this day Scaife's sister, Cordelia, will not speak to her brother.[5]

Right-Wing Family Values

Ever since Bill Clinton came into office, we've heard a lot of grandstanding from the Republican Party about the President's lack of "character." Although the guy has been married for over twenty years, successfully reared an intelligent and charming daughter, and managed the nation to its most prosperous and secure level in recent history, self-appointed moral leaders of the GOP have continually ascribed to him nefarious character traits. Well, what's good for the goose is good for the gander. Take a look at what these "moral beacons" of the right-wing party have on their records:

Paul Johnson: Conservative historian, ideologue, and author of the recent exercise in historical fiction *A History of the American People*, Johnson has made a career out of lambasting Democrats—and President Clinton in particular—for their purported "character deficiencies." This fellow, who argues in his latest book that

President Nixon was the victim of a coup by the liberal press, has also declared many times in print that liberals, progressives, and Democrats are people of weak moral fiber. Well, take a gander at this: As it turns out, this historical hack has been reported not only to be an adulterer, but also to have once smacked his wife in public, in the middle of a restaurant![6] If those are morals, buddy, I think I'll stay a sinner.

"*Lawsuit*" *Larry Klayman*: This guy, the ultimate Ken Starr wannabe, has accused the President of all kinds of demented crimes, including concealing evidence that former Commerce Department secretary Ron Brown was shot. Like Inspector Starr, Klayman has been living off the largesse of conservative nut Richard Scaife. (According to *The Nation*, Klayman has received $550,000 from Scaife.)[7] And, like his idol, Klayman has created a cottage industry out of investigating the President. At last count, he was spearheading eighteen separate lawsuits against the Clinton administration and dispersing subpoenas like most farmers spread manure.

This lawsuit-lover has even prepared a lawsuit *against his own mother* claiming she owes him for nursing care he provided for his late grandmother. When Klayman's brother was asked to comment, he found his sibling's behavior "disappointing," but was afraid to say more for fear of (you guessed it) a lawsuit. I guess to Lawsuit Larry, the family that's sued together is glued together.

OUTRAGEOUS BILL BENNETT

Bill Bennett is one of the Republicans out there who every now and then has something to say. Bob Bennett, his brother and the President's counsel in the Paula Jones case, is a great guy *and* a great lawyer. My problem is this: Because a guy has a great brother and a few great ideas, I usually conclude that he would have some knowledge of American history.

That's why I'm so perplexed by page 85 of Mr. Bennett's recent diatribe, *The Death of Outrage*, in which he declares that my attacks on Kenneth Starr are "unprecedented ad hominem attacks against an officer of the court."[8] What the heck is this guy talking about? Has he completely lost his mind?

Either out of naïveté or stupidity, Mr. Bennett doesn't seem to realize that his philosophical ancestors—rabid right-wingers of the South—were nailing "Impeach Earl Warren" signs all over Louisiana during my youth and accusing the Supreme Court of being in the clutches of Communism, Zionism, Race-mixingism, and God knows whatever ism they could think of. He also seems to forget that most district attorneys in this country have to run for reelection and are continually subjected to thirty-second commercials and attacks from political opponents. Moreover, Bennett completely ignores the many Republican attacks on independent counsel Lawrence Walsh during his tenure investigating Iran-contra.

Perhaps if Bill Bennett spent less time being sanctimonious and contemptuous and more time reading up on his American history and the First Amendment, he would be less likely to make asinine, historically inaccurate, and downright goofy pronouncements in his attempt to rehabilitate the GOP's top hatchet man.

If Bennett wants to talk about outrage, I wouldn't mind discussing why he and his cronies gleefully encourage the federal government to trample constitutional rights and liberties on a regular basis and then cry foul when someone wants government to help the poor feed their children or to offer medical care to the elderly. Now, that's really outrageous.

Conclusion:

The People v. Ken Starr

Now that you've had the chance to read through all the outrages I've written about, I guess you might get the sense that Ken Starr's baseless, insipid investigations have left me, well, a little irritated. But Miss Nippy always taught me to be an optimist, and to recognize that there's a silver lining to most things in life. Now you might well ask: James, old friend, where could there possibly be any good to all of the injustice and unfairness that the President's enemies and members of a vindictive press have put this country through? I may not be the legendary Mr. Ripley, but, Believe It or Not, I can answer that question.

For starters, Ken Starr has made absolutely sure that he will be the last person ever to be given this kind of unchecked power. His obsessiveness and abusiveness have served to remind all Americans of that classic lesson from history, my mother, and Lord Acton: "Power tends to corrupt and absolute power corrupts absolutely."

Ken Starr started out as the classic sort of Washington suck-up whose biggest sin in life was trying to please the rich and powerful. If you spend any time at all in Washington, D.C., you bump into these guys on every street corner. Only after becoming independent counsel did he turn into the dangerous, obsessive, anti-constitutional equivalent of a forensic Peeping Tom. We'll undoubtedly read about this creature in future history books, footnoted right beside his direct ancestor, Joe McCarthy.

The truth of the matter is, America should have known better. The independent counsel statute, an outsized reaction to Watergate, is a sorry example of what happens when you try to replace the political process with the best intentions of misguided, do-gooder journalists and Ivory Tower law professors.

Even true legal giants like Archibald Cox and Leon Jaworski were appointed to their posts not as a result of a binding statute, but as a result of the normal political process. Yet, like the potion that transformed Dr. Jekyll to Mr. Hyde, the independent counsel statute mutated an average, low-down, money-grubbing cigarette lawyer into a sex-obsessed, out-of-control, self-righteous, downright repugnant Inspector.

All Americans should hope and pray that we never see his kind again.

Another good to come from this whole seedy episode is that it will force the mainstream press to ask itself some very tough questions. Mainly, how could so many be so wrong about something so important? What caused them to be so utterly taken in by

Whitewater, Paula Jones, Ken Starr, and the rest of these so-called scandals? How could they have allowed themselves to become part of a cycle of such cynical gullibility, in which gluttonous major news organizations gleefully broadcast any unsubstantiated allegation against the President that Ken Starr and his henchmen could dish out?

*　　*　　*

Folks, to be honest, I didn't really want to write this book. I was hoping to—and still plan to—write *Five Smooth Stones*, a much more optimistic, upbeat tome that promotes progressive policies and tackles ideas, not individuals. I prefer the old school of politics, where you prove your enemies are fools, not criminals. And so, no, I didn't *want* to write this book, but there're the books you want to write and the books you *gotta* write. And when a poisonous tide rises unjustly against the President and his family, I can't stand mute. I've got to stand against it.

In a funny, queasy way, I feel lucky to have known Ken Starr. Because when a guy appears on the scene promoting all the big-monied interests and intolerant fools I've always detested, and representing damn near everything that's *ever* been wrong with politics, I feel privileged to go up against him. It's my own kind of holy war, but unlike Ken Starr's, it's a righteous one.

You know, people always ask me if there's anything I don't like about President Clinton. To tell the truth, there's not much: I think he's a superlative President and a wonderful human being. That said, of course he's disappointed me a few times over the years. I think it was wrong of him to sign a bill that took away the benefits of legal immigrants, who work so hard to make it in this country. I think his administration should have fought harder for Dr. Henry Foster, a man who's devoted his life to preventing teen pregnancies, as candidate for surgeon general. And I definitely think that, to his own harm, the President has a tendency to be far too accommodating to his political enemies. And I'll tell you this, although I agree with the President's politics 97 percent of the time and my wife's politics about 3 percent of the time, there's nothing on this Earth that would make me abandon either one of them.

*   *   *

Good people, it comes down to this: Whatever you think of William Jefferson Clinton, we can't lose sight of the fact that he's been viciously, maliciously, and rabidly attacked since the first day of his administration, not just by ultraconservative ideologues, who don't know much of anything, but by supposedly impartial journalists, who should know much better. Just as I'll be forever proud about having worked on the President's election campaign in 1992, I am equally proud to stand up for him during this pig-headed right-wing assault that has disintegrated into a two-bit sex show. Watching events play out during the tortured course of this "investigation" has been like having front-row seats to a freak show at the world's worst country carnival. And I tell you, I'm sick to death of it, the American people are sick to death of it, and it's time for Ken Starr, his hard-right Republican flakes, and his sycophant stenographers in the press corps to understand that they've

 ...And the Horse He Rode In On

done their high-profile butchering for the sake of shameless partisan gain and the sleazy lure of cheap personal glory.

My dear friends, we don't just have a wonderful country: We have the greatest nation on God's green earth. But somehow or other, we trusted the law professors, the Washington insiders, the so-called independent counsel, and the commentators to look out for America's best interests, and, quite simply, they failed. But rather than succumbing to the corrosive cynicism and mistrust of politics that their blundering has created, we must reenergize ourselves for the future. We need to get involved, fight back, speak out, and appeal once again to what is honest and good about America.

In sum, we need to put Ken Starr, the minions who do his bidding, and his wretched investigation forever behind us and appeal once again to what Abraham Lincoln, a truly great Republican, deemed "the better angels of our nature." It's our country, folks; these jokers just think they run it.

Appendix A:

*Who Got Paid by Whom to Say
and Do What*

You know, I never figured myself to be much of a fortune-teller. But if you look at my track record lately against the journalists, editorialists, reporters, columnists, and sycophants (aka JERKS) of the Washington establishment, you might want to start rubbing my dome for good luck. I don't know much, folks, but when it comes to seeing straight through these ridiculous scandals, I seem to have that clairvoyant Cajun mojo.

When all of the JERKS were drooling over the sordid tale of Paula Jones, I said that it was really about three things and three things only: money, money, and more money. As it turns out, I and about ten other people were dead-on out of the starting blocks and hundreds of the say-anything, print-anything media herd were dead wrong. Jones had *such* a strong case that Judge Susan Webber

Wright killed it before it could even go to trial and waste more of the American people's time, money, and patience.

Then, when the JERKS latched onto Whitewater as *the* scandal that would bring down the President's administration, those same ten other people and I told everybody what a baseless, just plain stupid digression this cockamamie land deal would turn out to be. Lo and behold, $40 million later it turns out that, once again, we were right and they were wrong.

When I was the first to speak out against Ken Starr and his sorry-ass investigation, the JERKS once again ran around in circles yelping at the fire. For months on end, the Georgetown cocktail set branded me with all sorts of epithets and publicly disdained my motives for impugning the integrity of the nation's foremost cigarette lawyer. (Here's a challenge for all you schoolkids: See if you can use the words "integrity" and "cigarette lawyer" in the same sentence in a positive way that makes sense. I'll give you a hundred years.) Well, guess what, folks? The JERKS have finally caught up with the rest of the nation and figured out what an out-of-control, biased, self-obsessed persecutor Ken Starr is at his cold stone core.

Paula Jones, Whitewater, Ken Starr . . . you know, you'd think that after a guy like me goes three-for-three against the JERKS' baddest pitches, he might be able to pack his bags and retire to the country to spend more time with his wife and daughters. But I don't think I've hit a home run yet—and no one really gets anywhere by hitting triples. (Ever heard of Sam Crawford? He's major league baseball's all-time triple leader. His name doesn't really ring up there with Aaron, Mays, Mantle, or the Babe, does it?)

So, I'll tell you what my four-bagger is, and you real JERKS out there may want to listen closely. Here goes: *In the next few years, we're going to find out that a lot of people were paid pailsful of money to tell bucketloads of lies.*

I'll bet you dollars to doughnuts that most of the allegations made about the President are a result of ultraconservative right-wing payoffs, funneled by conniving Clinton-haters to well-trained liars. The constant refrain you'll be hearing from me in the months, maybe years, to come is this: "Who got paid by Whom to say What?" (The three Rs have always been important, but these three Ws just pulled into second place right behind 'em.) Trust me, folks: This old, beaten-up, battle-weary Cajun is rounding third and heading for home, spikes high Ty Cobb–style if that's what it takes to get all the way there.

Take a look at these recently disclosed facts and foul connections that reinforce my view. Numbers just don't lie. Here's a humble accounting of money that's flowed from anti-Clinton sorts into "disinterested" and oh-so-respectable presidential investigations.

From Richard Scaife to the Arkansas Project:	**$1.7 million** **(in tax-exempt money!)**

From Ken Starr's investigation to David Hale:	**$68,000**

The Starr Investigations:[1]	
Contract Services	$2,215,161
Compensation	$8,847,163
Travel	$4,333,523
FBI	$14,429,739

The Troopers

Peter Smith, a six-figure contributor to Newt Gingrich's GOPAC, spent $80,000 to publicize sexual misconduct allegations against President Clinton. This money was used in part as research funding for David Brock, who was to dig up dirt on the President. It also included $6,700 in payments to Arkansas state troopers Larry Patterson and Roger Perry and a $6,600 payment to their lawyer, longtime Clinton adversary Cliff Jackson, paid after Patterson and Perry had told their "story" to David Brock.

Moreover, these two troopers were also paid an undisclosed sum by the Citizens for Honest Government, a conservative organization with ties to Jerry Falwell that promoted the *Clinton Chronicles* video. The CHG allegedly paid over $200,000 to various individuals making anti-Clinton allegations.

David Hale

The Justice Department is now scrutinizing the Arkansas Project, Richard Mellon Scaife's $1.7 million effort to discredit President

Clinton. This money was channeled through two Scaife tax-exempt foundations into the tax-exempt foundation that runs *The American Spectator* magazine. Most important, a bait shop owner named Parker Dozhier claims he was paid $35,000 by the Arkansas Project to clip local newspapers relating to Whitewater. However, his former girlfriend, Caryn Mann, her seventeen-year-old son, Joshua, and two anonymous sources on the *American Spectator* staff all claim that the Arkansas Project gave Dozhier much more than that. The money, according to these four sources, was used in part to make frequent cash payments to Whitewater "witness" David Hale, ranging from as little as $40 to as much as $500. Moreover, Dozhier purportedly leaked grand jury testimony to *Wall Street Journal* writers Ellen Pollock and Bruce Ingersoll. The founding editor of *The American Spectator* resigned in protest over the Arkansas Project. A few writers, including well-known neoconservative writer P. J. O'Rourke, joined him.

Paula Jones

Although Paula Jones promised in 1994 to give all proceeds of her litigation to charity, it turns out she's made quite a bit of pin money herself during the course of this case. Although she stated in her direct-mail letter that all donations were "going to help my legal case," it turns out she's already stashed $100,000 worth of donations in a private bank account; none of it has gotten anywhere near her lawyers. (Indeed, the Rutherford Institute, the right-wing group that helped Jones with her case, has publicly complained about this situation.) Moreover, Paula Jones, under the terms of a November 1997 contract with the direct-mail agency, is guaranteed at least $200,000 more.

Some of Jones's so-called litigation expenses have included a $2,000 shopping spree (for lookin' good and feelin' good in court), a $2,800 computer, and a $95 kennel for her dog. Moreover, according to a story in the *Chicago Tribune*, Jones's lawyers concede that the Paula Jones Legal Defense Fund's taxes may have been mishandled and underpaid.

In another fascinating, but ultimately unsurprising, development, a $50,000 donation to the Paula Jones Legal Defense Fund is reported to have been made by the Fund for a Living American Government (FLAG), a tax-exempt conservative foundation whose head, William Lehrfeld, is allegedly also the primary legal counsel to Scaife's Arkansas Project!

Appendix B:

More Opinions on Ken Starr

If you've gotten this far in the book, you might be starting to suspect that I'm none too fond of the independent counsel. But don't just take my opinion as gospel on the man. Here's what a load of other people have been saying about the esteemed Mr. Starr.

William Ginsburg, Monica Lewinsky's Former Attorney

"Repeatedly during discussions with the office of the prosecutor [Ken Starr] we have been squeezed. . . . They've even made threats to involve her parents, who, as far as I know, know nothing about the situation."[2] Moreover, his methods, while legal, are "ethically troubling."[3]

"After he [Starr] had the wire material, he lured Miss Lewinsky into the Ritz-Carlton Hotel in Pentagon City and, with the help of four or five FBI agents and three or four U.S. attorneys, managed to detain her—although she was technically free to go—for eight or nine hours [of questioning] without an attorney."[4]

The Brookings Institution's Stephen Hess

"I find it [the taping] very sleazy and close to entrapment. . . . [Starr's investigation] is a long way from what he was asked to do . . . and it strikes me that it gets more and more partisan."[5]

Former Justice Department Adviser Cass Sunstein

"I think the office of independent counsel has made him [Starr] nutty and I don't understand it. This kind of fishing expedition makes him not a Whitewater special prosecutor, but a general persecutor of the President."[6]

CNN Legal Analyst Roger Cossack

"I think there certainly is at least a hint of a political motivation [in Starr's actions], if not more. I think he clearly wants a conviction in this case. You cannot spend the amount of time and the amount of money that he has spent in this case—$25 million . . . without wanting to win. He wants to win. He wants to get the President.

"I mean, the thought of wiring up this young woman to go in there and try and get the goods on Vernon Jordan, a very revered

man in this country, as well as the President of the United States . . .
it really goes to show you how much Kenneth Starr wants this case
to come out his way."[7]

CNN Legal Analyst Greta Van Susteren

"There's so many other lawyers in this country. Why in the
world did we have to select someone [Starr] to investigate the
President of the United States who has such a strong Republican
agenda? Huge mistake to pick Ken Starr, so it certainly has the appearance that, indeed, it is political. You know, the Court of Appeals should have been smart enough to pick someone else. . . .

"[I]t appears that Ken Starr and Paula Jones's lawyers may be
working together. There seems so much symmetry in terms of
their requests. The interesting thing is that tomorrow, if she de-
clines to testify and does invoke Fifth Amendment privilege not to
testify, the question is will Paula Jones's attorneys be able to per-
suade Ken Starr to give her immunity. And once again, we'll see
whether or not they—there is this symmetry and just to what ex-
tent both sides may be cooperating against the President. . . .

"[Starr] did get tape recordings of Monica Lewinsky before he
went to the U.S. Court of Appeals for an expansion of authority.
That's unusual."[8]

Former Independent Counsel Lawrence Walsh

Asked if it was proper for Starr to wire Tripp: "I think it is very
doubtful that it was. I think that it was ill advised that after thirty-
odd million dollars spent investigating Whitewater, he ends up
policing the Paula Jones private litigation. I think it was bad judg-

ment if he was the one who initiated it. . . . It's beyond his jurisdiction. He had no duty. . . .

"Many prosecutors would think this is a risky area of investigation. . . . I don't understand the relevance of it."[9]

New York Times

"During his years as independent counsel, Mr. Starr continued private legal practice. He has also donated to Republican candidates and made speeches before groups antagonistic to Mr. Clinton, including one in 1996 sponsored by the evangelist Pat Robertson."[10]

CNN's Candy Crowley

"Beyond suggestions of a moral crusade, Ken Starr's other problem is critics who think his agenda is political. He was a Reagan Justice Department official who helped write the Reagan opposition to the independent counsel law. Starr went on to the Court of Appeals, but gave up his lifetime appointment to become George Bush's solicitor general. . . . Well into his fourth year as independent counsel, Ken Starr has spent about $30 million so far. With it, he has . . . come nowhere near the Clintons. . . . A year ago Starr wanted out, accepting a position at Pepperdine University. Big mistake: Critics said it showed Starr had nothing on the Clintons. . . . Worse, one of Pepperdine's big benefactors is a dedicated Clinton-hater who took out ads suggesting the late Vince Foster had been murdered. Both men denied they even knew each other, but it looked like a cozy deal. Starr did an about-face and stayed on."[11]

Newsweek's Evan Thomas

"He carries a lot of baggage. He's somebody who has been accused of, with some justification, partisan politics."[12]

Los Angeles Times

"Critics of the Whitewater probe have been many and loud here in recent months, as independent counsel Kenneth W. Starr's investigation passed the four-year, $30-million mark without bringing criminal charges against President Clinton, his wife, Hillary Rodham Clinton, or his top aides."[13]

Richard Cohen, Syndicated Columnist

"[W]e may wonder how an investigation launched some three years ago to delve into Whitewater turned into one concerning the President's sex life. Starr's charter has been so broad, and his funding so rich (more than $30 million spent so far), that he has been able to keep going when other prosecutors would have turned to more urgent matters. He is supervised by a friendly three-man appellate panel that appointed him in the first place. They are all, like Starr himself, staunch Republicans."[14]

Former Independent Counsel Michael Zeldin

"[Kenneth Starr] seemed to have discarded [his] mandate and gone into the political arena, which I think is the danger for him."[15]

Stephen A. Saltzburg, Reagan-Bush Deputy Assistant Attorney General, Criminal Division

"[Ken Starr's] logic is strained and feeds the feeling that the independent counsel may be biased against the President and has strayed far from the path that justified his appointment."[16]

Scott Turow, Lawyer and Author

"[Mr. Starr's] zeal [to take down Clinton], with little prospect of success, raises questions about his partisanship."[17]

ABC's Hal Bruno

"Instead of creating such a circus [with his remarks from outside his office], why didn't Ken Starr just hold a press conference?"[18]

The Wall Street Journal's Al Hunt

"[Ken Starr is a] tainted prosecutor. . . . He is a problem. Ken Starr ought to recuse himself from this part of the case."[19]

Time's Margaret Carlson

"Rabid prosecutor Ken Starr . . . is not an independent counsel—he's a partisan counsel. You can find people without a political axe to grind."[20]

Don Baer, Former Clinton Communication Director

"Starr's investigation has gone from a prosecution to a persecution. What was Ken Starr doing on a fishing expedition? This is a very serious moment in our history brought on by an unfettered prosecutor."[21]

Journalist Brit Hume

"A lot of people will find this [Starr's behavior] distasteful—the President will gain strength over these aggressive dirty-pool tactics."[22]

John Douglass, Former Federal Prosecutor, Iran-Contra

"[On Starr's *amicus* brief in the Paula Jones case] what's ... troubling is why he was representing the women's organization in that regard and doing it without pay.... If he or his law firm had an interest in promoting that point of view, the next question is 'Why?' Do they have an interest in presidential immunity, or is it because they are conservative Republicans and they like to see Clinton harassed?"[23]

Michael Johnston, Professor of Political Science, Colgate University

"Given his background before he was appointed, I think he is much more of a political figure than he would admit."[24]

Thomas Eisele, United States District Judge

"It is difficult to argue that Mr. Starr is not laboring under at least an appearance of conflict."[25]

...And the Horse He Rode In On

Bernard Lewinsky, Father of Monica Lewinsky

"What is going on, and what Ken Starr has brought upon her, is unconscionable in my mind. . . . To pit a mother against her daughter, to coerce her to talk—to me it's reminiscent of the McCarthy era, of the Inquisition, and even, you know, you could stretch it and say the Hitler era."[26]

Camille Paglia, Intellectual-at-Large

"At this point, most Americans would probably prefer being governed by a charming, oafish philanderer [President Clinton] than by a simpering, shilly-shallying, fascist milquetoast like Special Prosecutor Kenneth W. Starr, who has a face like creamed corn and the brains to go with it."[27]

David Duchovny, aka Agent Mulder of The X-Files

"I think Mulder is the worst FBI agent in the world. He spends millions of dollars investigating these paranormal phenomena and never comes up with any evidence. He's the Kenneth Starr of the FBI."[28]

Jerome Shestack, President of the American Bar Association

"If polls and the press are indicative, it seems that the public is questioning the impartiality and motivation of the independent counsel. . . . What should be done if we encounter a public loss of confidence in the counsel whose very work was to instill public confidence? . . . Are prosecutors entitled to ignore ethical prescriptions on the grounds that their pursuit of truth justifies departure from professional standards? . . . [When the independent counsel] is perceived as prosecuting the office more than the crime then the question arises whether the prosecutor is truly impartial."[29]

Gore Vidal

"Starr is now the most visible agent of corporate America wielding a new weapon under the sun: endless legal harassment of a twice-elected president so that he cannot exercise his office as first magistrate. . . . I should not in the least be surprised if yet another 'conspiracy' in the name of 'We the people' were to be set in motion against Starr for his willful and malicious attempt to overthrow two lawful elections reflective of the people's will and if [Starr] were to be put promptly on trial for treason against the United States and its people."[30]

Appendix C:

Sixty Reasons Why I Don't Trust Ken Starr's Investigation

1. Starr was appointed by conservative judge David Sentelle's panel after Sentelle's lunch with right-wing Clinton-hating North Carolina senators Jesse Helms and Lauch Faircloth.
2. Judge Sentelle's wife went to work for Senator Faircloth's office five months after Starr's appointment.
3. Starr wrote a friend-of-the-court brief about Paula Jones for the Supreme Court.
4. Starr wrote a friend-of-the-court brief on behalf of the Republican National Committee for Bush attorney general Richard Thornburgh.
5. Starr held Monica Lewinsky without a lawyer for eight or nine hours.
6. Starr tried to force Marcia Lewis, Lewinsky's mother, to testify against her. (She became ill as a result.)

7. Starr's investigators were bearing guns when they interrogated Lewinsky's brother.

8. Starr tried to pressure Whitewater witness Steve Smith to testify falsely, according to Smith.

9. Starr threatened Whitewater witness Sarah Hawkins with indictment without evidence of any wrongdoing.

10. Starr subpoenaed a sixteen-year-old boy at his school to intimidate him.

11. Starr subpoenaed Robert Weiner for making a phone call from his home.

12. Starr kept Susan McDougal locked in jail for eighteen months and tried to get her to testify to an imaginary affair.

13. Starr subpoenaed White House aide Sidney Blumenthal for talking with the press about his investigation.

14. Starr subpoenaed a Little Rock home decorating store where Webster Hubbell shopped.

15. Starr subpoenaed bookstores where Monica Lewinsky shopped.

16. Starr has subpoenaed Secret Service agents to testify against the President.

17. Starr leaks like a sieve, in an attempt to maximize harm to his potential targets.

18. Starr tried to dig up dirt on the President's sex life long before the Monica Lewinsky allegations.

19. Starr wired Linda Tripp *before* asking for authority to pursue those allegations.

20. Starr pressured Lewinsky to wear a wire *before* asking for authority to pursue further allegations.

21. Starr sought out a book deal with Newt Gingrich's agent, Lynn Chu.
22. Starr was co-chairman of an unsuccessful Republican congressional campaign (Kyle McSlarrow, 1994).
23. Starr considered running for a Republican Senate nomination in Virginia.
24. Starr maintained his million-dollar-a-year private law practice while working as independent counsel.
25. Starr represented Big Tobacco while working as independent counsel.
26. Starr's law firm, Kirkland & Ellis, was being sued by the Resolution Trust Corporation while Starr investigated the RTC.
27. Starr represented International Paper, which had sold land to the Whitewater Development Company.
28. Starr sits on the board of the conservative Washington Legal Foundation, funded by Big Tobacco.
29. Starr's investigators harassed White House Interior Department liaison Bob Hattoy about recruiting gay people to work in the Clinton administration.
30. Starr spoke at right-wing televangelist Pat Robertson's Regent University while working as independent counsel.
31. Starr spoke at the Richard Mellon Scaife–funded Property Rights Group while working as independent counsel.
32. Starr accepted a Scaife-funded tenured chair at Pepperdine University.
33. Starr pushed a Whitewater story as a member of the *ABA Journal* editorial board.

34. Starr performed legal work for the conservative Bradley Foundation.

35. Starr contributed $5,475 to Republican political candidates in the 1993–94 election cycle.

36. Starr contributed $1,750 to a political action committee that gave money to 1995–96 GOP presidential campaigns.

37. Starr has described no fewer than ten "critical stages" of his Whitewater investigation that never amounted to anything.

38. Starr's lieutenant Michael Emmick is a notoriously vicious prosecutor.

39. Starr's lieutenant Hickman Ewing is also a notoriously vicious prosecutor.

40. Starr's lieutenant Bruce Udolf violated someone's civil rights with his prosecutorial excess.

41. Starr's lieutenant Jackie Bennett says he "didn't know" Mickey Kantor was the President's personal attorney.

42. Starr contributed to a *New York Times Magazine* article to promote his investigation.

43. Starr himself has admitted that he has exercised bad judgment.

44. Starr has maintained both Washington, D.C., and Virginia grand juries, so that he can berate black witnesses in front of a white jury.

45. Starr has tried to breach the attorney-client privilege of Vince Foster, Monica Lewinsky, and President Clinton.

46. Starr has spent nearly $40 million to smear the President and has found nothing.

47. Starr's key Whitewater witness, David Hale, may have been paid by right-wing operatives.

48. Starr's key Whitewater witness, David Hale, is a liar.
49. Starr's investigation gave David Hale more than $60,000 for living expenses.
50. Starr's Whitewater state trooper witnesses were paid by Jerry Falwell.
51. Starr has been accused of shielding perjury in a General Motors case.
52. Someone at Starr's private law firm, Kirkland & Ellis, faxed an affidavit from the Jones case to the *Chicago Tribune* before it was filed with the court.
53. Starr's star "witness," Linda Tripp, worked simultaneously with Starr's and Jones's lawyers.
54. Starr had gained detailed knowledge of Monica Lewinsky's sealed deposition in the Jones suit *within hours* of its completion.
55. Starr has ties to right-wingers James Moody and George Conway, the Jones/Tripp lawyers.
56. Starr appeared on radio programs to speak in support of Paula Jones's case against the President.
57. Apparently for partisan political reasons, Starr withheld his report on Vince Foster's suicide until after the 1996 elections.
58. Starr, according to journalist David Brock, is a mainstay at right-wing parties.
59. Starr resigned before completion of his Whitewater probe, only to come back after intense right-wing pressure.
60. Starr was forced by Associate Attorney General Webb Hubbell to stop representing Bell Atlantic.

Appendix D:

Starr Gets Both Feet in His Mouth

Those of you who read my last book, *We're Right, They're Wrong,* know of the tremendous influence *To Kill a Mockingbird* had on my life. So you can probably guess how hopping mad I became when I heard Ken Starr compare himself to Atticus Finch in a recent speech. How horrific it must be for Harper Lee to hear the esteemed Inspector, an unabashed trampler of constitutional rights, try to evoke a comparison between himself and Atticus Finch. Better than I can ever say it, David Kendall, the President's lawyer and my friend, had this to say in a *New York Times* op-ed about Starr's literary pretensions:

Hands Off Atticus Finch!!!

I have been silent in the face of many provocations, but Independent Counsel Starr's attempt yesterday in a speech to a Charlotte, N.C., bar group, to co-opt Atticus Finch, hero of *To Kill a Mockingbird,* is too much. Perhaps I should have spoken out when Judge Starr tried to claim the mantle of Jack Webb (Mrs. Webb had some thoughtful and pungent comments on that comparison). But the attempt to make Atticus Finch, paragon of the fearless defense lawyer, into a prosecutor's docile and cooperative poster child simply will not do.

Atticus, a white lawyer in a small Alabama town during the Depression, defended his client Tom Robinson (a black man charged with raping a white woman) fearlessly, skillfully, and energetically in the face of community hostility. A humane skeptic, Atticus knew that "truth" was not the sole possession of the district attorney's office, that the procedural protections of the Bill of Rights belong to even the most unpopular of defendants, and that it was the defense lawyer's duty to defend his client against a hostile world.

One can only imagine what would have happened if the Office of the Independent Counsel had brought the charges against Robinson:

- Robinson would have been detained and questioned by the OIC and not allowed to talk to Atticus;
- Atticus's notes of his conversations with Robinson would have been subpoenaed;
- Atticus's daughter, the inimitable Scout, would have been subpoenaed (at her elementary school) and hauled before the OIC's grand jury, where she would have been grilled about her playground comments calling the prosecutors "racists";
- Robinson's purchases of reading material at the local Bible store would have been subpoenaed;
- The local newspaper would have been full of prosecutorial leaks from the prosecutors detailing all the other crimes Robinson was *really* guilty of;
- Robinson's old girl friend would have been suborned by the OIC and sent in for a friendly jailhouse visit, wearing a wire.

Last but not least, Atticus would have been hectored by the prosecutors and their apologists at every turn for blocking the "truth" by insisting on his client's procedural rights: "If we didn't believe the rape charge was true, we'd never have indicted him!"

No, it won't do. Atticus was game, he was knowledgeable, and he took to heart the obligation stated in old Canon 7—a defense lawyer should give a client a "zealous defense within the bounds of the law." If Atticus Finch were brought to life today, and moved from the dusty little Alabama county seat of Maycombe to a branch office in Washington, D.C., what would he be doing? He'd be championing some unpopular citizen hauled before a Congressional committee or representing some witness harassed by an overzealous independent counsel. He wouldn't be getting valentines from his opponents, but that wouldn't bother him.

Truth, as Atticus knew, emerges from the adversary system, by a vigorous defense as well as a vigorous prosecution. But Atticus was skeptical about human infallibility. His daughter remembers that his "most dangerous question" was always "Do you really think so?" In public life, a little skepticism—about our motives, our opponent's motives, even about our version of the "truth"—is an important safeguard for those who wield power. No true believer, Atticus Finch well understood that, in Justice Brandeis's words, "The greatest dangers to liberty lurk in insidious encroachment by men of zeal, well-meaning but without understanding."[31]

Appendix E:

Help Make Ken Starr's Life Easier

_____, 1998

Kenneth Starr
Independent Persecutor
Office of the Independent Counsel
1001 Pennsylvania Avenue
Washington, D.C. 20004

Dear Inspector Starr:
We all know that it's only a matter of time before you get around to subpoenaing everybody. Thus, I, _____, do freely admit and hereby affirm that I purchased a copy of James Carville's ...*And the Horse He Rode In On* at _____ on _____, 19__. In order to save you time and tax-payer money better spent elsewhere, I have enclosed my receipt from the bookstore. As you continue your investigations into the next millennium, I sincerely hope you will remember my helpfulness and abstain from delving into my private life and dragging my relatives into court when my time comes.

Best wishes,

Appendix F:

Questions for Ken Starr

Normally, the job of asking tough questions would fall to the independent press. But since our national media, for the sake of continued gigantic ratings, has universally decided to side with Ken Starr against the President, our normally intrepid cadre of Washington journalists have been silent as snakes. Meanwhile, Starr's boys have been throwing around all kinds of zany questions, such as when they asked Sidney Blumenthal if the President has a sex addiction. So, if you don't mind *me* asking the tough questions for once, Mr. Starr, what have you got to say for yourself on these matters?

1. How many attorneys have you hired during your tenure as independent counsel?

2. How many of those attorneys have quit?

3. What percentage of your lawyers have been African-American? What percentage of your lawyers have been Hispanic or Asian? What percentage of your lawyers have been women?

4. How much money have you made since you were named independent counsel? How much of that money was paid by America's taxpayers? How much is from your "part-time law practice"?

5. Your so-called ethics adviser, Sam Dash, told you there was nothing wrong with keeping your day job while the taxpayers are paying you at the same time. How much have you paid Mr. Dash in taxpayer money to advise you that it's okay for cigarette companies to pay you thousands of dollars while you're supposed to be doing the public's business?

6. We already know that when you subpoena White House aides, you always ask them about political strategy. We also know that you leak to reporters whenever you get the opportunity. How many times have you violated Rule 6E of the Federal Rules of Criminal Procedure by sharing this information with Newt Gingrich, Dan Burton, and other GOP political hacks?

7. Do you know how many people have accused you of demanding that they or their clients commit perjury for the sake of your vendetta against the President? (Just to refresh your memory: the names Steve Smith, Susan McDougal, and Mark Geragos should ring a bell here.)

Appendix G:

Now, most people believe that where there's smoke, especially if it's combined with the heat of flash bulbs and a legion of hungry pundits, there must be fire. But back in Miss Nippy's kitchen it was a different story. Most often smoke just meant brisket for dinner. Here, as promised, a recipe guaranteed to satisfy even the insatiable hunger of the most partisan independent counsel:

BRISKET

Chamber cooker or smoke box*
8–10 lb. trimmed brisket with thick fat on one side

---

* I use the Tierman Son-of-a-Brisket made by some folks out of Amarillo, Texas (1-800-753-1538). They provided this recipe.

> *2–5 T. dry rub (mix together equal parts salt, pepper, and paprika)*
> *Salt*

Set up cooker in smoking configuration.

Light charcoal and heat to 225 F. to 250 F.

Apply dry rub to both sides of brisket. Pat dry rub into brisket. Place brisket in cooker, fat side up. Wait 15–30 minutes and put wood chunks in a smoker box. Cook for 4 hours, adding more charcoal as needed to keep temperature at 225 F. to 250 F. Add more chunks to keep smoke going.

After 4 to 5 hours remove brisket. Liberally salt both sides of brisket (about 2 tablespoons total). Double-wrap brisket in aluminum foil and return to cooker, fat side down, for another 4 to 5 hours at 225 F. to 250 F.

After you've wrapped the brisket in aluminum foil, you need to add charcoal to smoker box. No need to add any more wood chunks, as brisket is wrapped tightly in foil and the smoke won't get to the meat.

For variety you can use other ingredients in the dry rub—garlic, lemon pepper, or whatever you like.

Afterword:

The Starr Report

Well, folks, it must be a cold day in Hell. Over four years and 50 million dollars after he was first named Whitewater independent counsel, Kenneth Starr has finally delivered his long-awaited report to the American people. And after all the years of blather about Whitewater, Travelgate, Filegate, Fostergate, and all the other gates the GOP could think up to keep their hatchetman busy, what does the partisan persecutor have to show for all the time and taxpayer money he spent on the public dole? Sex.

That's it. Sex. After all of Mr. Starr's high-minded reflections on the truth, after all of the commentariat's dour discussion of possible "high crimes and misdemeanors," after all the hype and hoopla surrounding the independent counsel's possible findings, what are we left with? Four hundred forty-five pages of smutty gossip about the President's unfortunate, indefensible, yet ultimately personal liaison with Ms. Lewinsky. It seems that since Mr. Starr couldn't find (or create) any criminal behavior by the President, he's instead trying to embarrass him out of office. Or, as former independent counsel Lawrence Walsh put it, the Starr report "was intended to shock the American public, arouse the House and Senate and make it very difficult to defend the President. . . . You can rail against the President for sexual promiscuity but don't make a crime of it."[1]

Can you guess how many times Ken Starr mentioned Filegate in his 445-page sex report? Zero. How about Travelgate? Nada. Of all the other alleged misdeeds by the President, only Whitewater, allegedly the very foundation of the independent persecutor's investigation, makes it into the report . . . TWICE. Meanwhile, sex is mentioned a whopping 543 times! (To paraphrase *Newsweek* columnist Jonathan Alter, the same Republican Congress that voted last year to keep pornography off the Internet voted this year to put it back on!) Hmmm . . . 543 to 0. It doesn't take a Ph.D. to figure out what is really on Ken Starr's mind.

Not fairness, it seems. In order to prevent the President's lawyers from exposing his report for the long-winded and legally baseless hatchet job it is, Ken Starr *refused* to let the White House see his findings before he presented it to his Republican cronies in Congress. However, David Kendall and his staff were both well aware of the independent counsel's sexual obsession and well educated by his constant leaking, and thus they had a rebuttal ready even without Starr's 445-page gossip column. Once again, Mr. Kendall can tell the story better than I ever could—his rebuttal summary may not be as titillating as Starr's sex report, but it's sharp enough to cut right through the independent counsel's confused conflation of infidelity and illegality. I include it in its entirety for your edification and your enjoyment, and I highly recommend that you pass it along to any smug, smirking Republicans you encounter at your backyard barbecues and office water coolers.

Friends, this Starr report is the icing on the cake. I've been saying for four years now that Ken Starr is a partisan, sex-obsessed crackpot of a GOP hatchetman, and this 445-page sex report only cements that view for the history books. When future generations look back at our time and see how the independent counsel's sanctimonious dog-and-pony show and its probing into the President's private life have deflected our nation's and our President's attention from the very real problems erupting around the world, I can guarantee they'll make sure America never sees his like again.

Executive Summary

Summary of Key Points of the President's Case in Anticipation of the Starr Report

1. The President has acknowledged a serious mistake—an inappropriate relationship with Monica Lewinsky. He has taken responsibility for his actions, and he has apologized to

the country, to his friends, leaders of his party, the cabinet and most importantly, his family.

1. **This private mistake does not amount to an impeachable action.** A relationship outside one's marriage is wrong—and the President admits that. It is not a high crime or misdemeanor. The Constitution specifically states that Congress shall impeach <u>only</u> for "treason, bribery or other high crimes and misdemeanors." These words in the Constitution were chosen with great care, and after extensive deliberations.

2. **"High crimes and misdemeanors" had a fixed meaning to the Framers of our Constitution—it meant wrongs committed against our system of government.** The impeachment clause was designed to protect our country against a President who was using his official powers against the nation, against the American people, against our society. It was never designed to allow a political body to force a President from office for a very personal mistake.

3. **Remember—this report is based entirely on allegations obtained by a grand jury**—reams and reams of allegations and purported "evidence" that would never be admitted in court, that has never been seen by the President or his lawyers, and that was not subject to cross-examination or any other traditional safeguards to ensure its credibility.

4. **Grand juries are not designed to search for truth.** They do not and are not intended to ensure credibility, relia-

bility, or simple fairness. They only exist to accuse. Yet this is the process that the Independent Counsel has chosen to provide the "evidence" to write this report.

5. **The law defines perjury very clearly.** Perjury requires proof that an individual knowingly made a false statement while under oath. Answers to questions that are literally true are <u>not</u> perjury. Even if an answer doesn't directly answer the question asked, it is not perjury if it is true—no accused has an obligation to help his accuser. Answers to fundamentally ambiguous questions also can never be perjury. And nobody can be convicted of perjury based on only one other person's testimony.

6. **The President did not commit perjury. Most of the illegal leaks suggesting his testimony was perjurious falsely describe his testimony.** First of all, the President never testified in the Jones deposition that he was not alone with Ms. Lewinsky. The President never testified that his relationship with Ms. Lewinsky was the same as with any other intern. To the contrary, he admitted exchanging gifts with her, knowing about her job search, receiving cards and notes from her, and knowing other details of her personal life that made it plain he had a special relationship with her.

7. **The President has admitted he had an improper sexual relationship with Ms. Lewinsky.** In a civil deposition, he gave narrow answers to ambiguous questions. As a matter of law, those answers could not give rise to a criminal charge of perjury. In the face of the President's admission of his relationship, the disclosure of lurid and salacious allegations can

only be intended to humiliate the President and force him from office.

8. **There was no obstruction of justice. We believe <u>Betty Currie testified</u> that Ms. Lewinsky asked her to hold the gifts and that the President never talked to her about the gifts.** The President admitted giving and receiving gifts from Ms. Lewinsky when he was asked about it. The President never asked Ms. Lewinsky to get rid of the gifts and he never asked Ms. Currie to get them. We believe that Ms. Currie's testimony supports the President's.

9. **The President never tried to get Ms. Lewinsky a job after she left the White House in order to influence her testimony in the Paula Jones case.** The President knew Ms. Lewinsky was unhappy in her Pentagon job after she left the White House and did ask the White House personnel office to treat her fairly in her job search. He never instructed anyone to hire her, or even indicated that he very much wanted it to happen. Ms. Lewinsky was never offered a job at the White House after she left—and it's pretty apparent that if the President had ordered it, she would have been.

10. **The President did not facilitate Ms. Lewinsky's interview with Bill Richardson, or her discussions with Vernon Jordan.** Betty Currie asked John Podesta if he could help her with her New York job search which led to an interview with Bill Richardson, and Ms. Currie also put her in touch with her longtime friend, Mr. Jordan. Mr. Jordan has made it clear that this is the case, and, as a private individual, he is free to offer job advice wherever he sees fit.

11. **There was no witness tampering. Betty Currie was not supposed to be a witness in the Paula Jones case.** If she was not called or going to be called, it was impossible for any conversations the President had with her to be witness tampering. The President testified that he did not in any way attempt to influence her recollection.

12. **There is no "talking points" smoking gun.** Numerous illegal leaks painted the mysterious talking points as the proof that the President or his staff attempted to suborn the perjury of Monica Lewinsky or Linda Tripp. The OIC's spokesman said that the "talking points" were the "key" to Starr even being granted authority to investigate the President's private life. Yet in the end, Ms. Lewinsky has apparently admitted the talking points were written by her alone [or with Ms. Tripp's assistance], and the President was not asked one single question about them in his grand jury appearance.

13. **Invocation of privileges was not an abuse of power.** The President's lawful assertion of privileges in a court of law was only made on the advice of his Counsel, and was in significant measure <u>validated</u> by the courts. The legal claims were advanced sparingly and as a last resort after all attempts at compromise by the White House Counsel's office were rejected to protect the core constitutional and institutional interests of this and future presidencies.

14. **Neither the President nor the White House played a role in the Secret Service's lawful efforts to prevent agents from testifying to preserve its protective**

function. The President never asked, directed or participated in any decision regarding the protective function privilege. Neither did any White House official. The Treasury and Justice Departments independently decided to respond to the historically unprecedented subpoenas of Secret Service personnel and to pursue the privilege to ensure the protection of this and future presidents.

15. **The President did not abuse his power by permitting White House staff to comment on the investigation.** The President has acknowledged misleading his family, staff and the country about the nature of his relationship with Ms. Lewinsky, and he has apologized and asked for forgiveness. However, this personal failing does not constitute a criminal abuse of power. If allowing aides to repeat misleading statements is a crime, then any number of public officials are guilty of misusing their office for as long as they fail to admit wrongdoing in response to any allegation about their activities.

16. **The actions of White House attorneys were completely lawful.** The White House Counsel attorneys provided the President and White House officials with informed, candid advice on issues raised during this investigation that affected the President's official duties. This was especially necessary given the fact that impeachment proceedings against the President were a possible result of the OIC's investigation from Day One. In fact, throughout the investigation, the OIC relied on the White House Counsel's office for assistance in gathering information and arranging interviews and grand jury appearances. The Counsel's office's

actions were well known to the OIC throughout the investigation and no objection was ever voiced.

This means that the OIC report is left with nothing but the details of a private sexual relationship, told in graphic details with the intent to embarrass. Given the flimsy and unsubstantiated basis for the accusations, there is a complete lack of any credible evidence to initiate an impeachment inquiry concerning the President. And the principal purpose of this investigation, and the OIC's report, is to embarrass the President and titillate the public by producing a document that is little more than an unreliable, one-sided account of sexual behavior.

Where's Whitewater? The OIC's allegations reportedly include <u>no</u> suggestion of wrongdoing by the President in any of the areas which Mr. Starr spend four years investigating: Whitewater, the FBI files and the White House travel office. What began as an inquiry into a 24 year old land deal in Arkansas has ended as an inquest into brief, improper personal encounters between the President and Monica Lewinsky. Despite the exhaustive nature of the OIC's investigation into the Whitewater, FBI files and travel office matters, and a constant stream of suggestions of misconduct in the media over a period of years, to this day the OIC has never exonerated the President or the First Lady of wrongdoing.

And Finally . . .

One of the great Democratic events in this country is Senator Tom Harkin's steak fry, held every September in Indianola, Iowa. Every year you can count on it being an absolute blast, with great folks and great Democrats eating well and having fun.

This year, Senator Harkin honored me by having me as the featured speaker of his steak fry, held on September 13, 1998. I thought I'd share with you a transcript of my remarks made before the people of Iowa and their wonderful Democratic senator. Enjoy.

I recently talked to somebody who drove through the north-central part of Iowa and he said that they've got a lot of hogs. He told me he got up early the morning after the Starr report went to Congress and the Republicans had gotten hold of the report and made a bunch of copies. They were throwing them onto people's lawns up there, thinking that would do Starr some good, when a hog got out and was kinda resting in a ditch. And so these Republicans came by and ended up throwing this report in the ditch right next to the hog. And the hog got up and started walking away, and the guy stopped and said, "Let me ask you something, hog. Why did you get up?" And the hog looked at him and said, "In these parts we're known by the company we keep." Even a hog has standards!

Folks, back there in Washington, all of the smart people—the pundits, the columnists, the commentators—have a big headache. They don't know what to do. They're complaining, "Look, out here in America people are supporting this President and sixty-eight percent think he's doing a good job. What's going on? These guys don't know whether to wind their rears or scratch their watches. They're sitting around their roundtables and panel discussions and they're saying, "These people out in America, they support Bill Clinton, and the GOP keep dumping this stuff, and they keep supporting Bill Clinton? We don't understand this! We told them five hundred times to stop supporting Bill Clinton but they just keep supporting Bill Clinton! Something is wrong with the people!"

No! Nothing is wrong with the people. You see, we know what happened. We remember twelve years of Republican rule! We saw a $3 trillion debt! We saw them defy this country! We were sickened by their assault on American families! We saw values and the minimum wage deteriorate! We saw wages stagnate! We didn't just see these things—we felt them!

Finally, after twelve years, the people of America had had enough. And we said, "We're going to do something. And we're gonna fight back because we love this country, and we care about the people who live in it, and we care about our traditions, and we care about the virtues of this country." And together we got behind this man who said if he were elected he would focus on the economy like a laser beam: "I'm going to get things done. We're going to do something about this deficit. We're going to help families, we're going to build schools, we're going to fight crime, we're going to go back to work and make this the kind of country we want to be proud of!"

...And the Horse He Rode In On

And boy, did he go to work. The budget of 1993: the most significant piece of economic legislation in this country since the New Deal. The crime bill: 77,000 new cops already funded, going on 100,000, and the lowest crime rate in twenty-five years. The budget deficit when he took over was $270 million—it's now zero!

Bill Clinton didn't just keep his promises. He exceeded them. He promised that he'd cut the budget deficit in half, and he eliminated it. He promised to create 8 million new jobs, and he's already created 16.5 million new jobs. He promised to pass the Family and Medical Leave Act, and we have family and medical leave. He got the job done.

And you know what the GOP did? They investigated. They had this committee, they had that committee. They spent $5 million, $10 million, $50 million! They said it was about Whitewater, or Filegate, or Travelgate, or Hillary! They even took the First Lady down to the grand jury. We legislated while they investigated, and as the country kept getting stronger, the investigation kept getting weaker.

We saw it with our own eyes. Then, in the *fifth* year of this investigation—after all the pontificating and millions of dollars—they come up with what? Sex. After all this time! So, you look at our country and you see a stronger country, you see promises kept, you see a man and his family under assault since the day he took office, and you wonder, "This is what they want me to overturn an election for?!"

This is a good man. This is a superb President. He did a bad thing, so let's blame him for that, okay? Fine. Now that we've done that, who are we going to give the credit to for the 16.5 million new jobs?

For the balanced budget? Who are we going to give credit to for the lowest crime rate in twenty-five years? Who are we going to credit for the most stringent clean air and water regulations we've ever had? Who are we going to give credit to for the fact that every facet of our nation is stronger? Since we're ready and willing to give the President all the blame for this indiscretion, then we'd better be ready to give him credit for all the good things he's done for our country.

I'm not through with them yet. The Republicans put $50 million of taxpayer money into this investigation machine, and in the end it produced the Starr report. Oh, the Starr report, the GOP said, will be about serious crimes against the Republic. It will be a very somber and serious document, they pontificated. Well, do you know how many times Filegate was mentioned? Zero. Do you know how many times Travelgate was mentioned? None! And Whitewater? Well, I gotta be fair—they mentioned it twice. Do you know how many times sex was mentioned? Five hundred forty-three. The Republicans spent $50 million for a report that mentioned sex 543 times. Somebody do the math on that—that's about $100,000 a word!

They set up this whole machine to overturn the election. They want the tobacco companies to run the country again. They want to reverse the gains that we made. They want us to turn our backs on our President and our country, and they're mad because we won't do it. Well, I have news for Jesse Helms and Lauch Faircloth, who put pressure on that judge to appoint Ken Starr. I have news for those Republicans who want to railroad this President out of office, and I have news for Kenneth Starr. To paraphrase a Democratic speech made over one hundred years ago, you will not crucify this man on a cross of passion! You will not press down upon the brow of this nation a crown of hypocrisy! We will stop you.

There are many things the American people share in common, and one of the most important is a sense of fairness. You know what the OIC did? I'll tell you what they did—I've been in this political game a little while and I know how to do this—they boxed the report up and sent it over to Congress, and when the President's lawyers asked for forty-eight hours to see the report and respond to it, the OIC replied, "Oh, no, we can't do that." In any other case, a person under investigation gets to respond to the charges, so people get a chance to look at both sides. Starr and his Republican cohorts set it up so the President couldn't respond. We'll do all of these unfair things and the American people will just forget about their sense of fairness and turn their backs on the President.

That's what they tried to do! And they can't figure out all these polls that are coming out that say the American people are still a fair people. I mean, they went to all the trouble of installing this sex-obsessed pygmy of a public man who now desperately tries to salvage his tarnished reputation in history by sending an unjust, unfair, and uncouth report to Congress without even giving the President the chance to respond to it!

What's at stake here? Well, we've got major differences between the parties. We've got things going on right now in the Congress that are going to affect this country for a long time to come. Because the Congress passed the 1993 budget legislation without a single Republican vote, we now have a budget surplus. The President says we should take that surplus and secure the future of Social Security. We ought to be sure that the people who are part of this nation and who work every day will be taken care of in their old age. We want to make sure that our country's elderly can have the dignity and financial security to take care of themselves and live their lives. Newt Gingrich wants to take their money and give it away on tax breaks. The President has a proposal to hire 100,000 new teachers and increase standards in America. They don't want you to know about that. If the American people keep their head down and focus on this investigation, what happens to that money? Does it go to the elderly or does it go to their campaign funds?

You see, they want you to take your eye off the ball. They want you to be dispirited. They want you to stay home on Election Day. They don't want you to work the phones. They don't want you at the headquarters. They want to fool you into taking your eye off the ball so they can get their hands on that surplus. Folks, I'm begging you: Don't take your eye off the ball. Go to the coffee klatches. Fight for your candidates. Get your friends out to vote. Get your neighbors out to vote. Get your relatives out to vote. Get people you don't even know but share the same values as you out to the polls.

My friends, the Republicans think you won't know about the real fights going on, and they hope that you'll stop caring. Well, they don't know you. They want you to turn against the President and be a part of their investigation conspiracy. We the people are sick and tired of Republican dirty tricks. We are sick and tired of this nickel-and-dime sex investigation. We're not going to give up—we are going to stand by our President. We are going to fight for our policies, we are going to fight for what's right, and we are going to fight these Republicans with everything we've got!

Notes

Introduction

1. *Washington Times*, 12/9/96; *The Wall Street Journal*, 12/13/96; *U.S. News & World Report, Weekly Standard*, 12/16/96.
2. *Washington Times*, 11/28/96.

He Crawled from the Deep

1. *Larry King Live*, CNN, 6/4/97.
2. Gene Lyons, *Fools for Scandal: How the Media Invented Whitewater* (New York: Franklin Square Press, 1996), p. 66.
3. *Dallas Morning News*, 1/21/94.
4. *Los Angeles Times*, 1/21/94; *Newsday*, 6/23/89; Associated Press, 6/19/89, 6/23/89.
5. Federal Election Commission records. Robert Fiske also made a $1,000 contribution to William Barton Gray, a Democratic candidate for Senate.
6. *The Nation*, 3/18/96.
7. *Washington Post*, 8/12/94.
8. *Rolling Stone*, 3/19/98.
9. *Washington Post*, 11/3/94, 8/24/94; CBS News, 7/20/90; *Orlando Sentinel Tribune*, 7/21/90.

10. *Washington Post,* 3/19/96; *Roll Call,* 8/11/94.

11. *Esquire,* July 1997.

12. Associated Press, 8/12/94; *Legal Times,* 12/12/94.

13. *USA Today,* 3/26/96; *Wall Street Journal,* 3/27/96.

14. *Arkansas Times,* 12/27/96.

15. *Salon,* 2/24/98.

16. *The Nation,* 3/18/96.

17. *The New Yorker,* 4/22/96.

18. *Today,* NBC, 12/9/96.

19. *Time,* 6/22/98.

20. *The Nation,* 5/20/96.

21. CNN, 7/1/98.

22. *Washington Post,* 5/5/96.

23. COPS figure: COPS Facts, Officer Hiring Initiatives, 1993–95, Department of Justice, Office of COPS. The program funds 75 percent of the total salary and benefits of each officer over three years, up to a maximum of $75,000 per officer over three years ($25,000 per year), with the remaining match paid for by state or local funds. Teachers figure: Based on $35,000 per year per teacher for salary and benefits (Department of Education 1993–94 Schools and Staffing Survey).

24. *Nieman Reports,* Winter 1997.

25. *New York Times Book Review,* 8/4/96.

Follow the Money

1. *Salon,* 2/4/98; *Time,* 6/22/98.

2. *Salon,* 3/27/98.

3. *Arkansas Democrat-Gazette,* 4/14/96.

4. *Arkansas Democrat-Gazette,* 7/10/96.

5. *Arkansas Times,* 9/6/96.

Follow the Money 2

1. *Los Angeles Times*, 12/21/93.
2. *Nightline*, 12/21/93.
3. *Salon*, 3/24/98.

Starr Wars

1. *The New Yorker*, 4/22/96; *Los Angeles Times*, 3/28/96.
2. *Time*, 2/9/98; *Washington Post*, 2/3/98.
3. Reuters, 4/14/96.
4. *Dateline*, NBC, 2/3/98.
5. *Washington Post*, 6/25/97.
6. *Los Angeles Times*, 6/26/97; *Boston Globe*, 6/26/97; *The News with Brian Williams*, MSNBC, 6/25/97.
7. *Dayton Daily News*, 2/14/98.
8. *National Journal's CongressDaily*, 5/11/95.
9. *New York Times*, 6/6/98.
10. *Boston Globe*, 7/14/97.
11. CNN, 1/23/98.
12. *Los Angeles Times*, 2/13/98.
13. *New York Daily News*, 2/8/98; AP Online, 2/11/98.
14. *Newsweek* (online), 1/21/98.
15. *Washington Post*, 3/26/98.
16. *New York Times*, 3/8/98.
17. *St. Petersburg Times*, 2/6/98.
18. *The Wall Street Journal*, 6/25/98.

Just Following Orders

1. *Washington Post*, 2/3/98.
2. *Minneapolis Star-Tribune*, 5/4/98.
3. *The New Yorker*, 4/22/96.
4. *New York Times*, 5/10/98.

5. *Chattanooga Times*, 4/10/98; *Salon*, 4/20/98.

6. *New York Daily News*, 2/11/98.

What's the Frequency, Kenneth?

1. *Legal Times*, 2/2/98.

2. *Burden of Proof*, CNN, 1/28/98.

3. *Abuse of Power: The New Nixon Tapes*, edited with an introduction and commentary by Stanley I. Kutler (New York: The Free Press, 1997), pp. 10, 9.

4. Associated Press, 12/8/94; *The New Yorker*, 4/22/96; *The Nation*, 3/18/96.

5. *Newsweek*, 5/6/96.

6. *The New Yorker*, 4/22/96; *Albany Times*, 1/18/97; *The Tim Russert Show*, CNBC, 12/7/96; *Legal Times*, 11/11/96.

7. *CBS Evening News*, CBS, 1/14/97.

8. *Reliable Sources*, CNN, 1/19/97.

9. *Insight*, 11/6/95.

10. CNN, 12/4/94.

11. *Washington Times*, 10/19/94.

12. *Washington Times*, 11/20/95.

13. *Insight*, 11/13/95.

14. *Washington Times*, 1/15/96.

15. *Washington Times*, 11/6/95.

16. *Pittsburgh Tribune-Review*, 2/4/96.

17. *Los Angeles Times*, 11/24/94; *Washington Times*, 12/3/94.

18. *Washington Times*, 4/3/96.

19. *Washington Post*, 1/29/95.

20. *New York Post*, 1/27/98.

21. *New York Times*, 1/29/98.

22. *New York Daily News*, 1/29/98.

23. *Washington Times*, 1/29/98.

24. *New York Daily News*, 1/23/98.

25. Ibid.

26. *Washington Times,* 1/23/98, 1/27/98, 2/5/98.

27. *Washington Post,* 1/24/98.

28. Ibid.

29. *Washington Times,* 1/27/98.

30. *Washington Post,* 1/23/98.

31. *The Wall Street Journal,* 2/5/98.

32. CNN, 2/6/98.

33. *Salon,* 5/28/98.

34. *Brill's Content,* July/August 1998.

35. Ibid.

36. *The Nation,* 3/17/97; *Washington Post,* 3/3/97.

37. *Washington Times,* 2/2/98.

38. *Arkansas Democrat-Gazette,* 5/6/98.

The Rabid Watchdog

1. *International Herald Tribune,* 2/20/98.

2. *New York Times,* 2/1/98.

The President's Character

1. Gingrich speech to GOP, 4/27/98.

2. *Washington Times,* 8/11/92.

3. *Boston Globe,* 6/21/92.

4. *New York Times,* 7/21/90, 1/6/89.

5. *Newsweek,* 5/18/98.

6. *The Observer,* 5/17/98.

7. *The Nation,* 6/29/98.

8. William J. Bennett, *The Death of Outrage: Bill Clinton and the Assault on American Ideals* (New York: The Free Press, 1998), p. 85.

Appendixes

1. *U.S. News & World Report,* 5/25/98.

2. *New York Times,* 1/23/98.

3. *This Week with Sam Donaldson & Cokie Roberts,* ABC, 1/25/98.

4. *New York Times,* 1/23/98; Associated Press, 1/23/98.

5. *Newsday,* 1/23/98.

6. CNN, 1/22/98.

7. Ibid.

8. Ibid.

9. *Internight,* MSNBC, 1/21/98, as quoted in *Hotline.*

10. *New York Times,* 1/23/98.

11. CNN, 1/23/97.

12. *Larry King Live,* CNN, 1/22/98.

13. *Los Angeles Times,* 1/23/98.

14. *New York Times,* 1/23/98.

15. *Crossfire,* CNN, 1/22/98.

16. *New York Times,* 1/28/98.

17. Ibid.

18. *Washington Week in Review,* ABC, 1/25/98.

19. *Capital Gang,* CNN, 1/24/98.

20. Ibid.

21. *Fox News Sunday,* 1/25/98.

22. Ibid.

23. Associated Press, 1/28/98.

24. Ibid.

25. Ibid.

26. *20/20,* ABC, 2/19/98.

27. *Salon,* 7/7/98.

28. *Entertainment Tonight,* 7/10/98.

29. Associated Press, 2/19/98.

30. *Houston Chronicle,* 8/17/98.

31. *New York Times,* 6/2/98.

Afterword

1. *Philadelphia Inquirer,* 9/12/98.

... And the